GOLD
An Illustrated History

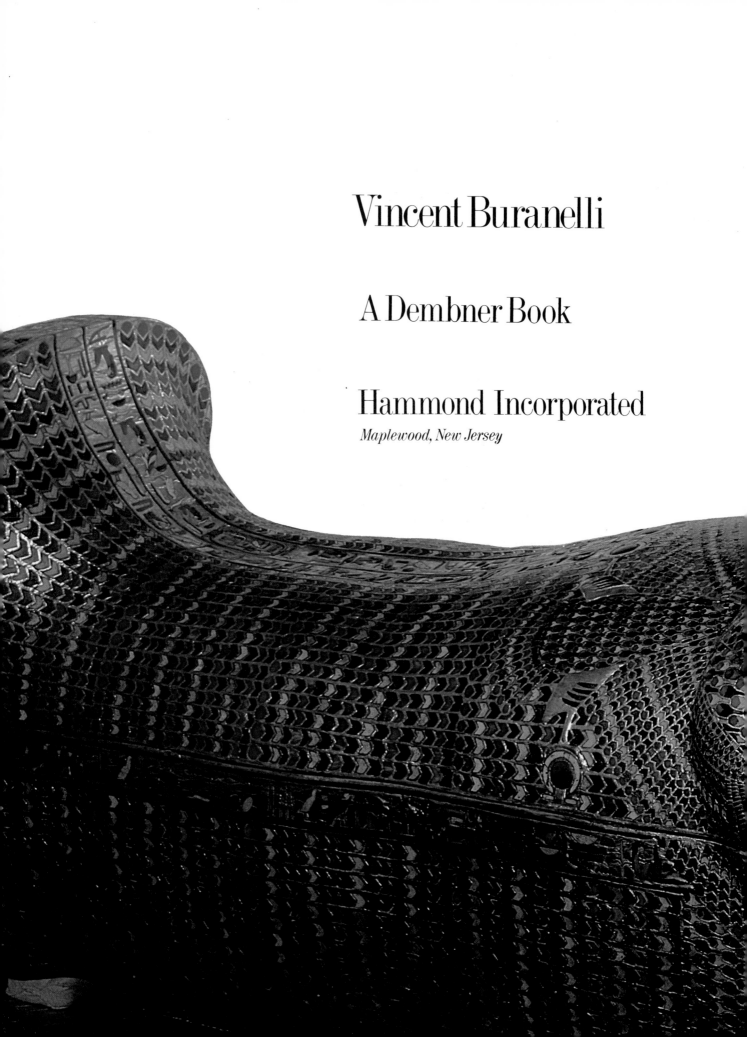

Vincent Buranelli

A Dembner Book

Hammond Incorporated
Maplewood, New Jersey

GOLD
An Illustrated History

Editor: S. Arthur Dembner
Executive Editor: Anna Dembner
Art Director: Judith Michael
Picture Editor: Laurie Platt Winfrey

Overleaf:
One of the great masters, Simone Martini,
executed this Annunciation in 1333 for the
chapel of S. Ansano in the Cathedral of Siena.

Title page:
Tutankhamen's second anthropoid coffin, made
of wood, carved, gold-plated, and decorated with
a beautiful design of multicolored glass paste, is
a fine example of the goldsmith's art.

Lines from "The Law of the Yukon" from
The Spell of the Yukon and Other Verses and
"L'Envoi" from *Ballads of a Cheechako*, by
Robert Service, reprinted by permission of
Dodd, Mead & Company, Inc.

LIBRARY OF CONGRESS CATALOGING IN PUBLICATION DATA
Buranelli, Vincent.
Gold: an illustrated history.
Includes index.
1. Gold—History. 2. Gold mines and mining
—History. I. Title.
TN420.B76   553'.41   79-13434
ISBN 0-8437-3136-2

Printed in the United States of America

Contents

Gold: An Illustrated History *by Vincent Buranelli*

Chapter One: Realms of Gold   8

Chapter Two: The Forty-Niners   36

Chapter Three: The Fossickers   68

Chapter Four: The Rise of the Randlords   88

Chapter Five: Over the Chilkoot Pass   106

Chapter Six: Smugglers and Thieves   138

Chapter Seven: Hidden Treasure   164

Chapter Eight: Gold Today   186

Gold in Literature   201

Acknowledgments and Picture Credits   217

Index   220

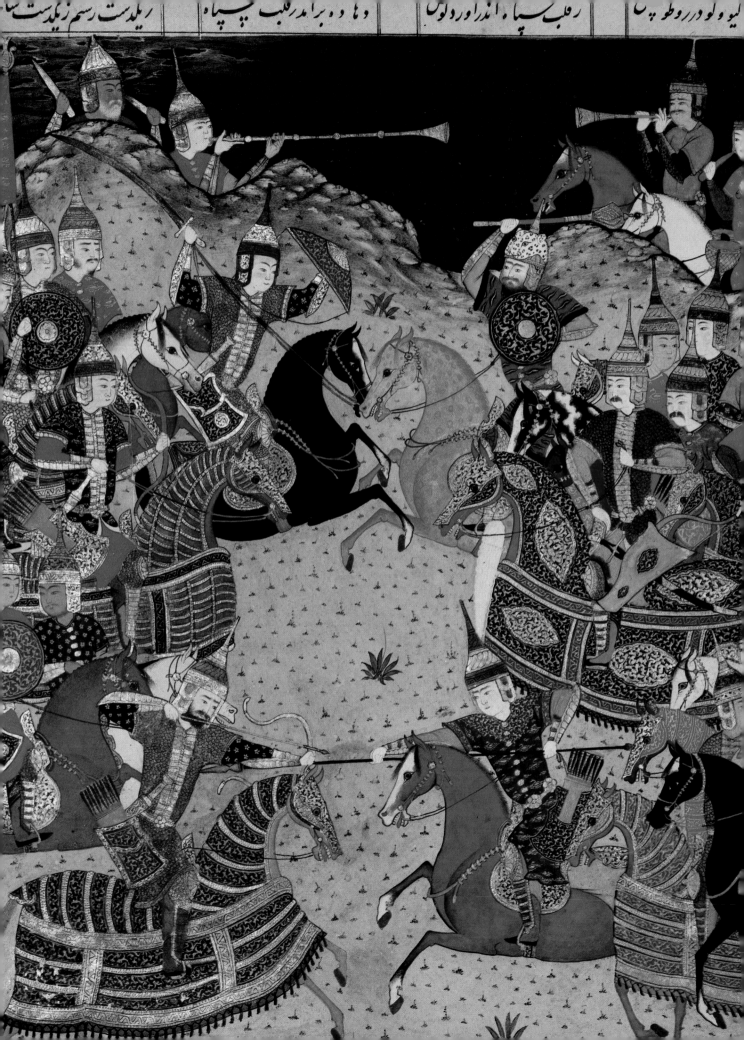

Chapter One

Realms of Gold

When the Pharaoh Tutankhamen, lying in a golden sarcophagus, surrounded by scores of gleaming golden artifacts, went to his tomb in Egypt's Valley of the Kings more than 3,000 years ago, humanity's romance with gold was already a long affair.

Somewhere in the world, when the world was young, the yellow metal first caught the eye of a human being—perhaps a flake shining in the sand at the bottom of a river in Europe, or a nugget uncovered by the wind in the soil of the Rand in South Africa, or a seam in a chunk of ore knocked loose by erosion in the Rocky Mountains, the Andes, or the Urals. We may imagine our prehistoric discoverer picking up this golden discovery out of curiosity, hefting it in one hand, turning it over and over, holding it up to see it shimmering radiantly in the sunlight.

Did he—or, one would like to think, she—feel at this moment that here was something worth keeping? Did the first symptoms of gold fever just then enter the blood of the human race?

However close to the truth this hypothetical scene may be, the fact is that gold *was* discovered and then rediscovered many times in many places on all the continents, for it is one of the commonest and most accessible of the metals. Nearly everywhere it became something to look for, to appropriate, to prize, and to display. The love of gold is one of the oldest of human passions, one of the deepest motives leading to art and culture as well as to battle, murder, and sudden death.

Adam and Eve before the Fall were immune to the temptations of the "land of Havilah, where there is gold" (Genesis 2:11), but their descendants have succumbed to the temptation so frequently that it is a recurring theme

This 16th-century Persian manuscript illumination (opposite) depicting a night battle, in gold and colors on paper, is from the Shahnameh (Book of Kings).

The alchemist's quest for gold was a serious matter, but these fanciful medieval woodcuts make us smile. We view (top) a man sowing gold coins in a field, and men dowsing for gold (bottom).

A 17th-century woodcut (opposite) is keyed to the twelve steps involved in making gold, culminating, the alchemist hopes, in item 12, "The Pieces of Metal."

throughout history. A poignant proof of what gold does to the human soul was found in the rubble of Pompeii—a petrified corpse still clutching a bag of gold after seventeen centuries, one possession the man would not leave behind when he fled in a panic only to be caught, asphyxiated, and buried by the cloud of choking dust and burning ashes with which the volcano Vesuvius overwhelmed the city.

Gold haunts our language in striking figures of speech—Golden Rule, Golden Age, Golden Years, Golden Opportunity, Golden Wedding, Golden Jubilee. The Golden Section of mathematics is the division of a line such that the entire line is to the larger segment as the larger segment is to the smaller. The *Golden Treasury* is a selection of superior poems in English. The *Golden Legend* is a collection of edifying lives of the saints. The *Golden Ass* is the sole surviving novel in Latin literature. The Golden Bough in Virgil's *Aeneid* protected Aeneas against the wraiths of the dead in Hades, and gave Sir James Frazer the title for a masterpiece of anthropology. When the Venetians registered their aristocracy, they listed the names in their Golden Book. When Emperor Charles IV revised the constitution of the Holy Roman Empire, he issued the new regulations in his Golden Bull. Prague is the Golden City. Istanbul has its Golden Horn, Pittsburgh its Golden Triangle, San Francisco its Golden Gate. Imagination has its Eldorado.

The desire for gold lies behind some of the most memorable events of all time. Queen Hatshepsut of Egypt sent trading expeditions down the Red Sea to the Land of Punt (unidentifiable today) to exchange gold for incense and other exotic products. King Solomon traded with Ophir (perhaps in Arabia) for "gold, and silver, ivory, and apes, and peacocks" (2 Kings 10:22). Submitting to the golden lure, the Greeks conquered Troy, the Romans conquered Spain, the Spaniards conquered Mexico and Peru. Coronado made his epic march through the American Southwest in search of the (nonexistent) Seven Cities of Gold. Sir Francis Drake circumnavigated the globe in the *Golden Hind*, keeping an eye out for Spanish galleons with cargoes of gold that might be his for the taking at the point of a sword. Forty-niners trekked across a continent because of gold in California. The prospectors who followed the Trail of Ninety-eight endured dreadful hardships in Alaska and the Klondike just for the chance to pan gold from the streams of the northern wilderness.

History's most persistent search for gold was a fantasy, the centuries-long effort by alchemists to find a way of transmuting the basest metal into the most precious—lead into gold. Alchemy began around 300 B.C. among the Greeks and Jews of ancient Alexandria, the first contributing scientific analysis, the second religious mysticism, to

IOÁNES
STRATENSÍS
FLANDRVS
1570

their common doctrine. Alchemy diminished during Roman times, flourished under the Arabs in the early Middle Ages, and reached its apogee in Europe during the late Middle Ages and the Renaissance, influencing Western thought until the eighteenth century.

Alchemy in its classical form was given two interpretations by its devotees, one higher or transcendental, the other lower or experimental. Transcendental alchemists held that the real objective of alchemical research was to gain a mystical vision of truth and righteousness. Experimental alchemists were content to seek for gold. The two vocations often went together, the combination being justified on the ground that there is an analogy between what happens on both levels—the transmutation of lead into gold is analogous to the transmutation of the soul from sin to virtue. As the saying went: "Divine grace is spiritual gold." Many alchemists therefore worked on both planes, devising a mystical theory that explained their labors in the laboratory, confident that in finding how to make gold they would at the same time learn how to achieve their own salvation. They looked down on the mere gold seekers, whom they called "puffers," men who blew their bellows on molten ore with no loftier inspiration than to turn base metal into gold.

The alchemists, judging by sheer hard work in the face of hope continually frustrated (for they were attempting the impossible), were among the greatest experimenters of all time. They tested theories as rigorously as do modern scientists, particularly their theory that sulfur (the principle of combustibility) and mercury (the principle of liquidity) are elements in all metals, each metal being basically a compound of the two in a special ratio. The art and literature of alchemy pictures the typical alchemist laboring day and night at his apparatus, feeding sulfur and mercury into his furnace, adding bits of gold, lead, and other raw materials, blowing up flames with a bellows, draining off steam and fluids into flasks and retorts, combing through the ashes, and eagerly testing whatever he come up with to see if he could catch the slightest golden gleam.

Alchemy had its own jargon, a lexicon of terms as mysterious to the uninitiated as those of modern science—athanor (furnace), aludel (condenser), alembic (part of a still), cupel (porous dish), pelican (vessel with arms for circulating liquids). Using his apparatus, the alchemist could experiment with incineration, calcination, coagulation, sublimation, and other laboratory procedures. The real problem of "the Art" was to try different ingredients and different ratios of ingredients that might suddenly produce the precise combination capable of causing transmutation. This hypothetical combination, known as "the Philosopher's Stone," was the will-o'-the-wisp that drew the alchemists on

A colorfully detailed painting (opposite) shows the philosopher-chemist meditatively observing his many assistants, who range from pink-cheeked youth to aged graybeard.

13

An alchemist's laboratory is shown in the details of this painting (above and right).

and on, generation after generation, into their prodigious labors. Some were financed by kings and nobles. Others were wealthy men indulging a whim. Still others were poor men galvanized by the thought of suddenly becoming rich.

The Philosopher's Stone never rewarded these tireless practitioners for the very good reason that transmutation was beyond the capabilities of alchemical techniques. The idea is feasible in today's subatomic physics, but the expense would be greater than the value of the transmuted gold.

Some alchemists claimed to have accomplished "the Great Work," but their claims are discounted for scientific reasons; in any case, no transcendentalist or puffer ever displayed the metallic fortune that would have been his had he succeeded. One class that pretended to have success in the Great Work was made up of charlatans and confidence men. Ben Jonson, Shakespeare's contemporary, wrote a burlesque of the type in *The Alchemist,* which is a play about a couple of rogues fleecing the greedy and the gullible who, completely taken in, are mesmerized by the thought of the gold that soon will be cascading from the alchemical apparatus in the makeshift laboratory.

In spite of failures and frauds, alchemy continued into the eighteenth century, the period of the Austrian empress Maria Theresa, the Russian empress Catherine the Great, and the Prussian king Frederick the Great, all of whom were interested in it as a potential source of national wealth. In the same century, Louis XV of France established a laboratory in the splendid château at Chambord for his official alchemist, the Count of Saint-Germain, who produced a few cloth dyes of a brilliant hue and nothing more, and was dismissed from the royal service.

The reference to dyes encapsulates the truth about alchemy. The alchemists did not transmute lead into gold, but they did lay the groundwork for chemistry, which emerged from alchemy like a butterfly from a cocoon. They contributed terms, techniques, and discoveries to the science founded by Robert Boyle in the seventeenth century and perfected by Antoine Lavoisier in the eighteenth.

Boyle repudiated the alchemical elements (sulfur, mercury, salt) in favor of an atomic theory of matter, and formulated Boyle's Law, which states that the volume and pressure of a gas vary inversely. Lavoisier demonstrated the conservation of mass when matter is transformed from one chemical state to another (e.g., water into steam), and he explained this fact in mathematical equations that the alchemists never heard of. Nevertheless, Boyle and Lavoisier were beneficiaries of the alchemists, as are the chemists of today. The alchemists' technique of cupellation, or using hot air to purify metal on a porous surface (the cupel), is still employed in metallurgy. The alchemists discovered ether and introduced the word *gas* into the language of science.

The pivotal figure was the Swiss alchemist Paracelsus, who, although he lived in the sixteenth century and reflected many old ideas now discredited, still had enough of the iconoclast about him to adapt alchemy to medicine. Interestingly enough, as a boy he lived in the Hapsburg province of Carinthia near the mines from which were taken iron, tin—and gold. These mines, run by the banking enterprises of the Fuggers, a wealthy German merchant family with headquarters in Antwerp, ranked among the most advanced of the time, and here Paracelsus saw how gold and other metals were removed from the ore, purified, and prepared for industrial use.

Later, after mastering alchemy, Paracelsus added salt (the principle of fixity) to sulfur and mercury as the third basic principle of metallic substances. His addition became a standard component of alchemical research, and he himself experimented with sulfur, mercury, and salt to see what medicinal properties he could discover, one of his conclusions being that a surfeit of sulfur in the body causes fever. Paracelsus discovered ether. From his teachings came the school of iatrochemistry, or medical chemistry, which presented alchemists with an alternative to transcendental alchemy or mere gold seeking.

Alchemy faded away, but not the craving for gold, which remained as strong as ever in the human psyche. Why is this? What gives gold its enduring fascination?

It is, to begin with, extremely beautiful, of a deep, lustrous color when pure, sometimes almost red and sometimes almost white when mixed with other metals, but characteristically of the "golden" hue that pleases the human eye so much. It stands out among all the metals because of its color, which it holds untarnished to an unparalleled degree in any climate, weather, or temperature. Gold always and everywhere looks like gold.

Again, it is the most malleable of metals, soft enough to cut with a knife, plastic enough to be worked into sculpture, firm enough to maintain its shape. The allied virtue is its ductility. A lump of gold can be beaten into plates so thin that, stacked up, they make hundreds to an inch. It can be drawn into a wire fine enough to be used in miniature electronics, reliable enough to be used in space-flight equipment.

Then there is the durability of gold. Virtually unscathed by time and use, by wear and tear, by sunlight, fire, or sea water, it is nearly indestructible. The gold of Tutankhamen is as bright now as when the Egyptian goldsmiths fashioned it. Older pieces of pristine freshness have been recovered by archaeologists from other sites. Metallurgists infer the

continued existence of primordial pieces that, having undergone many reworkings and transformations, are extant in modern artifacts from gold pins to gold teeth.

Gold is so durable partly because it resists chemical decomposition. Most acids have no effect on it. The leading solvent, nitrohydrochloric acid, was called *aqua regia* ("royal water") by the alchemists because it could disintegrate the royal metal.

Modern science knows much more about gold than the alchemists knew. Today gold is defined as an element of which the symbol is Au, the atomic number 79, the atomic weight 196.967, the melting point 1063°C., the density 18.88–19.4, and the hardness 2.5–3.

Geologically, gold is a product of titanic forces that twisted and buckled the crust of the earth eons ago. It customarily occurs in granite quartz, which it penetrated in molten form far underground, forming seams in the ore that catapulted upward under fantastic pressure from the surrounding subterranean materials. If it stayed below the surface, it has to be dug or mined. On the surface, it either remained in place in the ore, showing as seams, or was carried away by erosion, which often removed the rocky "shell" and left it on the ground as dust, flakes, or nuggets. Swept into rivers, it moved downstream, but not as quickly as rocks or stones, for, being one of the heaviest metals, even small pieces resisted when lighter detritus swirled along with the current. This type of gold can be recovered by washing or dredging, the placer methods.

The science of gold is interesting because it comes from the world of reality. The mythology of gold is interesting because it comes from the human imagination, which has never ceased to be dazzled by golden dreams.

The myth of Danaë concerns Zeus, the supreme god of the ancient Greeks, who had a penchant for seducing mortal women. Danaë was the daughter of Acrisius, King of Argus, who, warned by an oracle that she would give birth to a son who would kill him, locked her in a brass tower to which no man could gain entrance. Zeus, exercising a craftiness unbecoming in a resident of Mount Olympus, managed to reach her by metamorphosing himself into a shower of gold and falling into her tower through openings in the roof. Titian has painted a splendid picture of Danaë receiving Zeus in his golden disguise.

She gave birth to a son, Perseus, known from his origin as *aurigena* ("of golden origin"). Terrified, Acrisius had mother and child locked in a chest and thrown into the sea. The chest floated ashore, Danaë and Persues were saved, and he grew up to be a hero who, among other feats, killed the monstrous Gorgon, Medusa, whose hideous glare turned human beings to stone. Perseus approached Medusa safely

by looking at her in a mirror provided by Athena, and he was able to cut off the head of the monster with his sword. On his return, Perseus tried to be friendly with his grandfather, Acrisius, whom, however, he killed accidentally while throwing the discus, thus fulfilling the prophecy.

The myth of Midas is a cautionary tale, a warning against the dangerous consequences of desiring gold too much. Midas, king of Phrygia, in what is now Turkey, having done a favor for a friend of the god Dionysus and allowed by Dionysus to make one wish that would be fulfilled, wished that everything he touched might turn to gold. His desire came to pass. He ran his fingers over his house, furniture, china, tools, and weapons, and watched with delight their transformation into gold.

But when, forgetting his wish, he ordered a meal, the food and wine obeyed the decree of the god, and what he raised to his lips became uneatable gold. In despair, Midas prayed

Titian's Danaë portrays a beautiful young woman turning longingly toward the cloud from which Zeus comes to her in the form of a shower of gold.

17

for release from his fatal gift, whereupon Dionysus instructed him to bathe in the Pactolus River, which he did. To his immense relief the gold things around him resumed their natural forms. This bath of King Midas explained, for the Lydians, why gold was to be found in the bed of the Pactolus.

The story of Croesus, essentially true but embossed with legends, also comes from Asia Minor. It is the story of a king of Lydia who lived in the sixth century B.C. Croesus conquered Asia Minor from the Aegean Sea to the Halys River, and ruled in power and opulence from his capital city of Sardis. His gold was proverbial—"as rich as Croesus," the Greeks used to say.

Considering war against the Persians, Croesus consulted the Delphic Oracle, which informed him that if he went to war, a kingdom would be destroyed. Croesus, assuming this meant the Persian kingdom of Cyrus the Great, led his troops into battle and suffered the defeat that destroyed his own Lydian kingdom.

The quest of the Golden Fleece had a connection with reality in that the people of Colchis on the coast of the Black Sea "panned" their rivers by dipping sheepskins into the water, collecting the particles of gold that clung to them. This seems to have been the origin of the myth of the Golden Fleece hanging on an oak near Colchis and guarded by a fire-breathing dragon.

Commissioned to bring the Golden Fleece back to Thessaly with a kingdom for a reward, Jason and his Argonauts sailed for the Black Sea, where Medea, daughter of the king of Colchis, and a witch, protected them with her magical powers. She put the dragon to sleep and enabled Jason to wrench the Golden Fleece from the oak. He hastily embarked with the Argonauts for Thessaly, taking her with him.

Jason and Medea lived together until he announced his intention to marry a daughter of the king of Corinth, a revelation that triggered the barbaric passions of the witch from the Black Sea. She revenged herself by murdering the bride-to-be with a poisoned garment, then killing her children by Jason, after which she fled to Athens in a chariot drawn by dragons. Herodotus says she went from there to the Near East, where she gave her name to the land of Media. She has been re-created for contemporary theater audiences by Judith Anderson, who gave a searing performance in one of the most powerful dramas in world literature, the *Medea* of Euripides.

We enjoy stage performances of a different type in Richard Wagner's *Ring of the Nibelung*, a monumental cycle of four music dramas about the curse of gold when it is the object of cupidity. Kirsten Flagstad, the foremost Wagnerian soprano of the twentieth century, made the part

On a 5th-century krater, a Greek vase used for mixing wine and water, the nude Jason, protected from harm by Medea's magical powers, is shown reaching for the Golden Fleece.

of Brünnhilde an experience for those lucky enough to have heard her in opera houses around the world, notably at the Metropolitan Opera in New York City.

In *The Rhinegold*, a hideous Nibelung (gnome) steals the gold of the Rhine River from the Rhine Maidens (water nymphs) and makes it into a magic gold ring that causes fraud and violence among the gods. In *The Valkyries*, the king of the gods, Wotan, creates Brünnhilde, a woman warrior who is to be an instrument in ending the curse of the magic ring; but she betrays his trust and he puts her to sleep within a circle of fire to await a hero who can cross through the flames and waken her. In *Siegfried*, the hero who gives his name to the drama gains possession of the ring after killing the dragon guarding it, crosses through the flames, and awakens Brünnhilde. In *The Twilight of the Gods*, Siegfried is killed while wearing the ring, Brünnhilde immolates herself on his funeral pyre, and the Rhine rises over the ashes, allowing the Rhine Maidens to regain their gold as they retrieve the magic ring. The curse of the gold culminates in the destruction of Valhalla, home of the gods.

As basic as the golden theme in music and literature, and even more widespread, is the golden theme in art. The history of gold is as old as the history of human culture, for gold artifacts have been found in Stone Age graves from Ireland to Egypt, and the goldsmith has been an honored artisan since the pharaohs emerged into the light of history.

Gold coins alone are a key to the past, as they have been since the reign of Croesus, who started a tradition that would become permanent and worldwide—he had some of his gold minted into coins to be used as money. Persians, Greeks, Romans, Byzantines, Arabs, and others too many to mention followed him in this, and so did the United States until 1933 when, during the first administration of Franklin D. Roosevelt, the minting of gold coins ceased.

Gold is a witness to the fact that civilization in the West challenges that of the Near East in antiquity. The earliest carefully worked pieces of gold jewelry yet known, dating to about 3500 B.C., have been unearthed in Bulgaria, proving that metallurgy developed independently in the Balkans and ending the belief, axiomatic with prehistorians a generation ago, that Europeans learned how to work metals from the timeless lands across the Mediterranean. The newest methods of dating have pushed back the limits of European civilization, and little gold figurines from Bulgaria are prominent in the evidence.

The figurines are primitive in workmanship. Cattle, for example, are drawn naively in straight lines and rough semicircles, so that no one would call them either lifelike or abstract. But they plainly had a long artistic tradition behind them when they were fashioned.

The noble (above), an English gold coin, c. 1360, pictures a sailing vessel, while the Byzantine and early Christian coins (below) celebrate the portraits of dignitaries.

Making death masks of important people is an ancient custom. Egyptian Pharaoh Tutankhamen's mask (below), one of the most beautiful ever found, is crafted of solid gold with inlays of precious stones and colored glass. The pre-Columbian mask of embossed gold (above) was that of an unidentified wealthy man. The gold mask (right), often mistakenly called the Mask of Agamemnon, was discovered in the royal graves of Mycenae, Greece.

The greatest artists in gold of the ancient world were the Egyptians, who mined it in the desert and in Nubia, panned it from the Nile, and enjoyed the security and the time, and of course the genius, to turn their gold into one of the priceless treasures of our cultural patrimony. Goldsmiths in Memphis and Thebes wrought in gold solidly and yet in graceful lines, turning lumps of metal into rings, bracelets, brooches, earrings, necklaces, coronets, figures of gods and kings, and representations of abstractions such as the ankh (symbolizing life). The religious motif was fundamental because the Egyptians associated gold with the sun and with the sun-god, Ra.

The tomb of Tutankhamen, who died in 1352 B.C., surrendered the most remarkable of all gold collections, pieces large and small, ornate and plain, from the heavy golden sarcophagus to a delicate model of the deadly asp. Golden figurines of the pharaoh, sitting and standing, show him as a wizened little figure with a sad look on his face, just what one would expect in a realistic portrayal of the frail teenager (eighteen at his death) forced into a position too much for him, a captive of circumstances (he inherited the throne in the turbulence following the death of Ikhnaton, the heretic pharaoh), controlled by the general who was supposed to be his regent. So much gold for so insignificant a person!

The rival culture of the Near East, that of the Sumerians in Mesopotamia, developed a tradition of working in gold taken from the Tigris and Euphrates rivers. The royal graves at Ur, dating toward the beginning of the third millennium B.C., contained gold artifacts of a high sophistication. The Sumerians practiced human sacrifice when they buried their royal dead, and the "death pits" at Ur gave up a grisly trove of men and women who, voluntarily or otherwise, had been buried at the same time as their dead rulers.

The usual ornaments were in the pits—jewelry, cups, figurines—but two are of special interest. A gold dagger in a gold sheath has a meticulous balance of blade and hilt, and is wrought in precise lines. The other item is the famous "Ram Caught in a Thicket," so called because it seems an illustration of the biblical account of Abraham and Isaac. Could this be the ram Abraham sacrificed in place of Isaac? No it could not, for it antedates that scene by more than a thousand years.

Another great book, the *Iliad,* comes into the story of gold and art. Heinrich Schliemann, excavator of Troy, while digging at Mycenae on mainland Greece (1876–78), found a superb golden mask that he connected with the king of Mycenae who led the Achaean host to the conquest of Troy. Schliemann called his find the "Mask of Agamemnon." In his excitement, he reported to the king of Greece: "I have

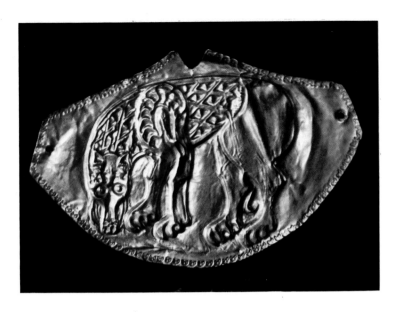

The warrior Scythians fashioned this gleaming ornamental gold helmet (opposite) in the 4th century B.C.

The Thracians, considered by the ancient Greeks to be war-like barbarians, created this beautiful stylized lion (top left) on a gold pectoral, and this solid gold drinking cup (top right) embellished with representations of the gods. The Greeks showed their craftsmanship and versatility in the fine gold comb (bottom).

looked on the face of Agamemnon!" Actually, he had looked on something much older, apparently the death mask of a king of Mycenae who reigned three centuries before the Trojan War.

Schliemann's passion for verifying the *Iliad* by the spade had already led him astray at Troy. True, he uncovered Priam's city, but it was the sixth city on the site, not the second as he thought, which, of course, being deeper under the debris, went back to an earlier epoch on the "windy plains of Troy." Having recovered a large cache of Trojan gold (nearly 9,000 items), Schliemann characteristically dubbed it "Priam's treasure." We know he was in possession of artifacts that were already old when Troy fell around 1200 B.C.

Gold is an indicator of artistic culture where one would hardly expect to find it. The Scythians were nomads of the steppes who wandered from China to the Ukraine during the centuries between the dominance of Assyria in western Asia and the conquests of Alexander the Great. Riding on horseback, living out of wagons, burying their dead along the trail, the Scythians left few things durable enough to last through the millennia. But they did leave gold artifacts, and in quantities sufficient to tell us that they were not simply barbarians.

Life was violent on the steppes, and animals were everywhere. The Scythians, consequently, specialized in scenes of predators rending their prey. We see in glistening gold the terrifying fury of lions killing horses, griffins killing stags, sinuous serpents wound around strange beasts in a death grapple, and even spiders in lethal combat with other insects.

There was also a peaceful side to the art of the Scythians. Their domesticated animals (horses, sheep, goats) appear at rest in exquisite miniatures. The household arts are rep-

resented by pins, needles, combs, bowls, trays, goblets, and pots. Personal ornaments are as common as with any other people. The Scythians did so much extraordinary work in gold that the Russians were able to mount a dazzling exhibition in 1975 at New York's Metropolitan Museum of Art.

Ancient Italy boasted the Etruscan goldsmiths, but the classical Greeks and Romans did little in this field compared to their other achievements. The Islamic peoples were hampered by the Koranic injunction against icons. Europe, however, revived the use of precious metals under religious inspiration. The Carolingian Renaissance under Charlemagne (742–814) saw the rise of a brilliant school of court goldsmiths who produced altarpieces depicting the lives of the saints and gold-leaf covers for the Bible.

The Carolingian impetus died down during the Age of the Vikings (roughly 850–1050). The Middle Ages followed, when goldwork, like most of Western culture, took an impress it has never lost. Religion continued to be a prime inspiration, and from Scotland to Sicily the altars of Catholic cathedrals gleamed in gold; but increasingly, secular ideas intruded. Royal crowns and coronets of the nobility began to be made of gold. One of the most ornate, dating from the fourteenth century and now in the Munich Residenzmuseum, is inlaid with enamel and precious stones.

Gold and pearls emphasize this cope fastening (above) depicting the Annunciation. Jewels embellish the Visigothic golden cross (right) created by this Germanic people who had sacked Rome and gone on to conquer Spain.

Constance of Aragon, wife of Holy Roman Emperor Henry VI, wore this gleaming gold and jewel-encrusted tiara (opposite).

Overleaf, left: This 10th-century Byzantine book cover, depicting the Archangel Michael, is an example of the splendor, power, and culture of the Empire, and explains the strong influence of its art forms in Italy, Sicily, Syria, Greece, Russia, and other Eastern countries.

Overleaf, right: In this illuminated gold page, an elaborately dressed Byzantine emperor presents the book to the seated figure of Christ.

Wealthy burghers and prosperous merchants commissioned special pieces for special occasions. The Lord Mayor of London wore a gold chain. In Burgundy, each knight of the Order of the Golden Fleece wore a miniature sheep made of gold. Many a cavalry general wore gold spurs.

Meanwhile, the Far East experienced a great era of goldwork under China's T'ang Dynasty (618-906). Persian goldsmiths brought to China the secret of beating gold into fine sheets, a key to working on a small scale since beaten gold is lighter than cast gold and therefore better adapted to objects for personal adornment. This method enabled Chinese goldsmiths to make delicate combs, brooches, and earrings for queens, princesses, and ladies of the nobility.

Marco Polo, the Venetian traveler who noticed nearly everything in China, found that along the south coast gold dust could be collected from the sands of islands facing the mainland rivers. He also noticed that Kublai Khan possessed so much of the precious metal that he awarded commissions to his generals in the form of golden plates on which the words of the commission were inscribed.

The Japanese, who turned gold into art early in their history, today possess an extraordinary example—a solid gold bathtub shaped like a phoenix with which a Tokyo hotel titillates its patrons.

India was rich in gold and in craftsmanship, and so it remains, Calcutta being a center of the art in all styles from realistic traditional to abstract modern. The aristocratic marriage custom continues of daubing the face of the bride with visible specks of gold dust. Even the less well off bedeck themselves or their homes with gold whenever they can afford it.

In Africa, one area of the far west produced so much gold that Europeans called it the Gold Coast. The kings of Ghana, the local name for the territory, wore solid gold caps as a sign of their regal sovereignty, a sight that astonished the Portuguese sea captains who anchored in the gulf and went ashore at Accra. Ghana does not produce gold in great quantities anymore, but golden objects from the past— rings, earrings, bracelets for wrist and ankle—are still common in everyday use.

The European Renaissance would be illustrious in goldwork if only because of one artist and one masterpiece, namely, Benvenuto Cellini and the golden saltcellar he made for King Francis I of France The large figures on the saltcellar are of the god Neptune (the sea) and the goddess Ceres (the earth). The smaller figures represent Night, Day, Twilight, Dawn, and the Four Winds. Ceres is flanked by a dog, Neptune by seahorses. Gold has never been carved more expressively than in the face on the stern of the boat holding the salt—a craggy, gnarled face, the brow con-

The graceful serenity of this 8th-century gilt bronze Buddha (opposite) shows the cultural and religious aspects of the powerful Chinese T'ang Dynasty.

The picaresque Benvenuto Cellini, Italian sculptor, metalsmith, and author, designed this superbly beautiful and incomparable saltcellar in the 1540s, one of the few of his works to survive to the present day.

Charles IX, King of France (1550–74), owned this magnificent and beautifully embroidered gold shield (opposite). Charles also owned responsibility for the massacre of 20,000 French Huguenots on St. Bartholomew's Day in 1572.

tracted into a stern frown, the eyes deep-set and piercing, altogether the countenance of a titan who has just come from Hades or the bottom of the sea.

Cellini in his memoirs is not the soul of veracity, but the reader may believe him when he says of his saltcellar that the king "exclaimed in astonishment and could not stop looking at it."

The goldsmiths of the Renaissance reinforced the trend toward secular subjects, devoting to palaces and their furnishings the labor that once had been nearly confined to churches. The Louvre in Paris possesses many examples— the gold helmet and shield that belonged to King Charles IX (reigned 1560–74), the mirror set in gold that Venice presented to Queen Marie de Medici of France (reigned 1600–31) at the time of her royal wedding, and others just as valuable.

France took the lead in goldwork and retained it into the eighteenth century. All over Europe goldsmiths flattered the French masters in the most sincere manner, by imitating them. Thomas Germain, an engraver for Louis XV (reigned 1715–74), did an enormous amount of fine work in gold, but unfortunately most of it was destroyed in the pillaging of the palaces during the French Revolution.

Ironically, some of Germain's best pieces survived the

Russian Revolution. Table sets commissioned by Russian nobles can be seen in Leningrad along with the work of other Western goldsmiths who were popular with men and women of the Tsar's court. These treasures help to explain the career of Peter Carl Fabergé, the Russian of French descent who became the foremost goldsmith of his time (1846–1920). Fabergé remains most famous for the golden Easter eggs he wrought for Tsar Alexander III (reigned 1881–94).

Part of the upsurge in goldwork after the Renaissance was caused by an influx of gold from the New World. Columbus discovered America—and American gold. The Great Navigator's report of golden ornaments on the bodies of almost-naked savages inspired other Europeans to follow in his wake during the Age of Discovery. Hernando Cortez, the conqueror of Mexico, and Francisco Pizarro, the conqueror of Peru, were prominent among them.

Cortez came first, in 1519. Montezuma, the Aztec emperor, attempted to fend off the invader by sending him golden gifts, including a large disk symbolizing the sun. This only made Cortez all the more determined to fight his way into the Aztec capital (Mexico City). As conqueror, the Spanish captain executed Montezuma, seized his gold, and ruled his empire. Cortez had fallen into disfavor when he died in Spain in 1547, but he had set an example for the next ruthless conqueror in the New World.

Pizarro found even more gold than Cortez did because the Andes provided the Incas with more of the precious metal than could be found elsewhere in the Americas. The Incas were the latest Peruvians to exploit the gold mines in the mountains, and they inherited traditions of goldwork from the Chimu, Mohica, and Nazca peoples. The Chimu were unsurpassed in the New World for putting human expressions into faces on their golden utensils and tools. The Incas specialized in gold for their temples because they, like the Egyptians, associated gold with the sun-god. The Inca tradition continued in full splendor until the coming of Pizarro and his Spanish conquistadors. Even after the conquest, the tradition continued in outlying areas of the mountains until it gradually waned and disappeared during the next century.

A noble culture was mutilated when Pizarro ordered a multitude of gold objects to be melted down in order to turn the metal into ingots of a standard size, thus making it easier to divide the spoils and transfer the gold to Spain. It was poetic justice that he did not enjoy the results of his vandalism for long. He was assassinated in Peru in 1541.

As the gold of the New World poured into the Old World in Spanish galleons, Europeans became more gold-conscious than ever. Economists developed the idea that in

Our Lady of Vladimir is a gold, enamel, niello, and jeweled icon from 17th-century Moscow.

order to be prosperous, a nation should own as much monetary gold as possible. The nations began to hoard

Peter Carl Fabergé, goldsmith and jeweler to the imperial Russian court, created this fabulous egg, shown with the golden coach designed to fit inside.

bullion, and to use economic wars and shooting wars to accumulate more of it.

The human passion for gold, as always, came through these tumultuous events undiminished. The eighteenth century gave way to the nineteenth, and still men and women desired gold for its own sake. The same is true today.

Among all the golden clues to history, none is more interesting than the gold ring, which symbolizes wealth, authority, or affection.

The idea of wearing a gold ring for ostentation probably occurred to someone shortly after the discovery that gold could be worked into different shapes. Wherever the goldsmith's art has been practiced—from Mesopotamia to Peru, from India to England—gold rings are found in archaeological digs. And in nearly all cultures, the making of gold rings for personal adornment has continued down the centuries into our own time. One difference between the present and the past is that the practice of wearing rings on all the fingers, common among wealthy Romans, is no longer popular.

The gold ring as a symbol of authority comes from ancient Egypt. The pharaoh or his chief minister wore a signet ring bearing the seal that, when pressed into wax, made a papyrus roll official, sealed it, and kept it from being unrolled and read surreptitiously. The ring of authority is mentioned in the biblical story of Joseph: "And Pharaoh took off his ring from his hand, and put it upon Joseph's hand . . ." (Genesis 41:42). Joseph then ruled Egypt in Pharaoh's name. This Egyptian usage was the origin of the signet ring worn by royal chancellors in medieval and modern Europe.

The gold ring as a symbol of affection is the one we are most familiar with. A number of ideas came together to create the modern wedding ring. First, there is the thought that the groom is giving the bride a valuable love token. Secondly, the ring forms a circle, and the circle has since early times represented union and unity because there are no ends that diverge. Thirdly, the circle represents eternity because it has no stopping point. In the religions of the West, love, union, and eternity are supposed to characterize marriage, and they all come together symbolically in the gold wedding ring. The groom slips it onto the third finger of the bride's left hand because in olden times it was thought that a vein ran from this finger directly to the heart. A ring today encapsulates that much of human history.

Gold rings have adorned the fingers of many men and practically all women of power, influence, authority, or position. Hatshepsut wore a gold ring, and so did Cleopatra, and Marie Antoinette, and the Dowager Empress of China, and every First Lady since Martha Washington.

The golden spires of the Shwe Dagon Pagoda (opposite), the most celebrated temple in Burma, dominate the skyline of the city of Rangoon.

A beautiful Indian bridesmaid wears every bit of jewelry she owns. Then she will hoard it, as a form of insurance, as Indian women have done through the ages.

Chapter Two
The Forty-Niners

John Augustus Sutter came from Switzerland—Roman Helvetia—and so, having made his way to California in 1839 and settled on a Mexican land grant in the Sacramento Valley, he dubbed his estate "New Helvetia." The locals, who had never heard of Helvetia and presumably were vague about Rome, called it "Sutter's Fort." It was an apt title because this was frontier country up near the foothills of the Sierras. Indians camped nearby, the nearest white neighbor lived a hundred miles away, and protection by the Mexican governor in Monterey was an agreed-upon fiction.

During the decade of 1839–49, Sutter created a virtual barony on nearly 50,000 acres. He had to build everything himself, support himself, protect himself, and he ran his establishment skillfully and authoritatively. He raised a rectangular adobe wall eighteen feet high and more than two feet thick, marked by embrasures from which cannon could bombard attacking parties that might be under the illusion that this isolated habitation was an easy conquest. A garrison, mainly of Indians, stood guard day and night, armed with rifles and swords. Sutter's pennon flew triumphantly over the compound.

Within the walls there were the necessities for a small, self-contained community—storehouses, workshops, bakery, mill, smithy, guardhouse, even a jail. Sutter occupied a two-story structure in the middle of the building complex, where servants waited on him and secretaries made reports and received orders.

Here he ranched, farmed, ran frontier industries (weaving, tanning), and distilled strong brandy from the grapes in his extensive vineyards. Here he also entertained lavishly the travelers, trappers, scouts, and military men (among them John C. Frémont and Kit Carson) who, after mounting

With a determined look on his face and all his possessions packed on his donkey, a gold prospector (opposite) sets out to seek his fortune.

James Marshall posed beside the sawmill where four years earlier, in 1848, his discovery of gold sparked the California gold rush.

the Sacramento River or descending from the high passes of the Sierras, craved his hospitality.

Debts accumulated because he had to meet a heavy payroll and because goods and furnishings were expensive to bring from the coast up the Sacramento to New Helvetia. Still, life was calm and enjoyable until a stormy January day in 1848 when a horseman galloping through mud, wind, and rain careened to a stop at Sutter's front door with a startling message that shattered the calm and transformed his life.

The rider was James Marshall, a wanderer from Lambertville, New Jersey. He was Sutter's partner in the construction of a sawmill at Coloma, to the northeast on the South Fork of the American River, forty miles or so from its confluence with the Sacramento at Sutter's Fort. The millstream at Coloma needed deepening before the wheel would turn, and each evening Marshall had the dam opened to let the water flow through; in the morning he would shut the gate and examine the bed of the stream to see where shallow spots had been evened out by the water and where his men would have to dig.

On the morning of January 24, 1848, a yellowish object in the water caught his eye. "I reached my hand down," he wrote later, "and picked it up. It made my heart thump, for I was certain it was gold. The piece was about half the size and shape of a pea. Then I saw another piece in the water. After taking it out, I sat down and began to think right hard."

Marshall was not a geologist who could on inspection differentiate between gold and pyrite, "fool's gold," and he did not trust his first impression. He decided on the spot to make one of the elementary tests for gold, the malleability test, which he did by hammering one piece out of shape. When it refused to break under the pounding, he surmised it must indeed be gold.

Gathering more pieces from the millrace, he carried them to his workers and explained where they had come from and what he thought they were. This was the first report of gold at Sutter's sawmill, the origin of the greatest gold rush of all time. Marshall's workers were the first to believe the report and prospect for more gold. They found it, as their foreman had, in the millrace.

More tests were made. A piece of the metal placed on a shovel and thrust into a fire of manzanita logs, the fuel used in smelting operations, emerged unscathed. Jennie Wimmer, the camp cook and a native of Georgia who had seen gold mined and tested back home, put one piece to a crucial test. She dropped it into a pot of boiling water laced with lye and left it on the fire for a day and a night. When she retrieved the piece, she found that neither the heat nor the acid had affected it in the slightest.

That was decisive for her and for everyone else at the sawmill. Malleable, durable, untarnishable, and heavy enough to be caught in the millrace—this had to be gold the South Fork was carrying down the American River. The number of discovered pieces had implications so enormous that Marshall saddled his horse, rode through dirty weather to Sutter's Fort, and reported to its master.

Marshall has left us an account of how he demanded secrecy. Then, alone with Sutter in his private room, Marshall took out a handkerchief, unfolded it, and revealed the golden contents. They put the metal through more tests, including the Archimedean test for specific gravity: Placing a pile of it on one scale, they balanced it with silver and dipped the scales in water. The yellow side sank down with the heaviness of gold.

Neither of the partners felt overjoyed. Coloma lay outside New Helvetia, so that Sutter could not claim ownership of the gold areas. Reports of the discovery would certainly cause him to lose his staff and probably bring gold seekers swarming into the area, making it impossible to build and operate his sawmill. New Helvetia itself would be endangered since the American River must be carrying gold down to the Sacramento, and strangers could not be expected to be overly scrupulous about respecting his private property.

Sutter's decision was to go to Coloma himself. There, he asked his workers to stay on the job until they finished the sawmill—and to keep silent about what they had found in the millrace.

John Augustus Sutter was troubled by debts relating to his 50,000-acre barony, and the discovery of gold there did not alleviate that condition.

This 1848 map shows locations of the upper gold mines along the South Fork of the American River.

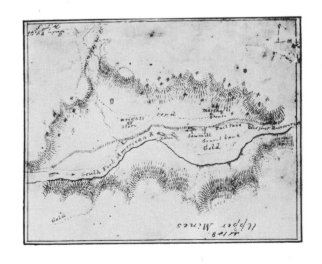

TAKE NOTICE.
Ho! for California!

A Meeting of the Citizens of
the Village of Canajoharie and its vicinity, will
be held at the house of T. W. Bingham, on

FRIDAY EVENING,

the 19th inst., at early candle light, for the purpose of taking into consideration the propriety
of forming a company to proceed to California,
and mining for GOLD. All who feel interested on the subject are requested to attend.
MANY CITIZENS.
Canajoharie, Jan. 16, 1849.

Citizens of Canajoharie, a village near Albany, New York, were urged to attend a meeting for the purpose of joining forces to strike it rich in California.

A sailing card (opposite, top) announced clipper-ship Enterprise's *proposed trip to San Francisco. The illustrations include not only the clipper ship but also a side-wheeler, a monitor, a balloon, one railroad train crossing a viaduct, and another crossing a suspension bridge.*

Poking fun at the pell-mell stampede to California, this 1849 cartoon (opposite, bottom) portrays then-futuristic forms of transportation—rockets and blimps—and a parachute, for safety's sake.

The first exhortation they took to heart; the sawmill began operating on March 11. The second lapsed immediately. The men found abundant quantities of gold around the Coloma area in their spare time. Inevitably they talked. Among the first to know were Sutter's hired hands at New Helvetia, who, as he had feared, began slipping away to the American River and its tributaries. As word spread, strangers came stampeding in—from Monterey and San Francisco, from along the West Coast, from Mexico.

American officials in California, a recent prize of the Mexican War, reported to Washington, and on December 5, 1848, President James K. Polk referred to the discovery in his annual message to Congress: "The accounts of the abundance of gold in that territory are of such an extraordinary character as would scarcely command belief were they not corroborated by the authentic reports of officers in the public service, who had visited the mineral district and derived the facts which they detail from personal observation."

That statement, heard throughout the nation and throughout the world, triggered the gold rush of forty-nine. It brought Americans to California from all over the country. It brought foreigners from every continent.

These were the modern argonauts whose golden fleece awaited them, not on the coast of the Black Sea, but in the streams of central and eastern California. One of them, David Rohrer Leeper, wrote a book on his experiences in the goldfields under the title *The Argonauts of 'Forty-Nine*. Bayard Taylor went to a different poetic image and called his memoir *Eldorado*. This word or the variant *El Dorado* ("the golden land") was applied to California itself, to the American River, to an area that became El Dorado County, and to hotels, saloons, and gambling dens around San Francisco and the mining towns.

The Argonauts bound for Eldorado from the East Coast of the United States, the point of origin for a large segment of the mass migration, had three routes open to them.

The first was by sea "around the Horn," heading south to Tierra del Fuego, through the Strait of Magellan, and then northward in the Pacific. This was the longest route, about 17,000 miles from Boston to San Francisco, with all the discomforts suffered by passengers incarcerated aboard ship during a voyage lasting usually about five months. There was seasickness to contend with, and monotonous days and weeks. Storms tossed the biggest ships to and fro, terrifying landlubbers who saw huge waves bearing down on them, heard and felt the ship's planks straining under their feet, and clung to the nearest nailed-down support to keep from going overboard.

Still, this route was familiar to Americans. For twenty

years, captains from Nantucket and New Bedford had been taking their clipper ships down the Atlantic and across the Pacific in the China trade. In 1840, Richard Henry Dana had published *Two Years before the Mast*, a sailor's realistic account of a voyage from Boston to San Francisco and back. So the passenger who sailed around the Horn did not have to fear the perils of pioneering into the unknown, nor, if his ship weathered the passage, did he have to exert himself beyond finding something to while away the time on board.

Shipping lines went all out to cut the time and set records. In 1851 the *Flying Cloud* made it from New York to San Francisco in 89 days under a driving skipper who kept her sails unfurled and her crew hard at work. Eventually steamships set much faster records, but by then the gold rush was past its heyday.

A sea and land route to the goldfields was by ship to the Isthmus of Panama, on foot across the isthmus, and by ship to San Francisco. This was the quickest route (usually within two months) but it was also the most dangerous, the one with the highest toll in human lives. Bayard Taylor, who went by way of Panama, noted the hazards—thick jungle, dismal swamps, heavy rain, bad air, poor food, yellow fever, cholera, dysentery, and guides who were maddening in their *mañana* attitude to travel. For crossing the isthmus, guides extorted about ten dollars a day from *los Americanos* desperate to be on their way to California. This was an immense sum for the time and place.

Bad experiences in Panama recounted by numerous American travelers contributed to the belief in Washington that a canal should be built across the isthmus in order to shorten and simplify travel between the east and west coasts of North America. Fifty years later, the idea became a reality. President Theodore Roosevelt used all his political power and diplomatic skill to start construction of the Panama Canal in 1904.

During the gold rush, another sea and land route lay across Mexico, a shorter voyage, but one that involved a longer trip overland.

But the classical route to the goldfields, the one most memorable in the epic of the gold rush, lay directly across the continent. It was the most time-consuming of all for anyone departing from the East Coast. The jumping-off point for the long haul west, Independence, Missouri, lay half a continent away from Boston, New York, and Philadelphia, and from there the worst half of the journey still lay ahead. But for thousands this was the choice.

The argonauts of forty-nine traveled across North America on foot, on horseback, in covered wagons, carrying with them as much clothing and equipment as they thought necessary to begin seeking gold. They often took too much

This map shows the dangerous overland route through Panama. The longer route across the United States, on horseback, in covered wagons, and even on foot, is depicted in this 1853 illustration (below).

Departing for California on February 20, 1849, the coastal freighter Hartford *(opposite) took on over 50 passengers in New York and, confounding the marine experts, arrived safely in San Francisco a year later.*

OFF FOR CALIFORNIA.

The comments in the bubbles of this cartoon and the illustrations show how gold fever brought out the worst in people.

Four sketches (opposite), made by J. Goldsborough Bruff as he led 63 men and 13 wagons across the Plains, demonstrate some of the rigors of the journey. From top to bottom we see (1) straggling travelers, (2) ferrying the Platt River, (3) mules bolting, after one wagon is upset, and (4) a difficult passage over a "stinking" Nebraska creek.

since Eastern businessmen had a vested interest in advertising everything from dried foods and cooking utensils to leather trunks for carrying gold to hand pumps that purportedly would simplify placer mining on the rivers. Greenhorns responded avidly to advertisements sprouting in the newspapers. One, in the New York *Daily Tribune:* "Instructions for collecting, testing, melting, and assaying Gold, with a description of the process of distinguishing gold from worthless ores, for the use of persons going to California."

Most of this equipment would have been useless in California. Most was abandoned along the way by their exhausted owners due to the rigors of the trek over plains, deserts, and mountains. One traveler, James Abbey, estimated that in the desert beyond the Humboldt Sink he saw abandoned property "to the value of at least $100,000 in about twenty miles."

Sarah Royce of New York made the transcontinental trek with her husband and baby daughter. Years later she wrote her recollections for her son, Josiah Royce, the Harvard philosopher, when he was gathering material for his history of California; and as she was a perceptive woman and had kept a "pilgrim's diary" of the journey, her account is one of the most authentic we have.

She tells of the family lurching across Iowa in a covered wagon through the dust, rain, and mud, with harrowing delays caused by the wandering of their untethered animals, and finally drawing to a halt at Council Bluffs on the Missouri River. Ferried across, the Royces joined a wagon train traveling together for safety's sake into the Great Plains where hostile Indians rode nearly at will and occasionally attacked white intruders disturbing their hunting grounds. Sarah Royce saw the ravages of cholera on the Elkhorn River and the perils of the shifting sands of the Platte.

Beyond Salt Lake City the trio from New York struck into the desert, where at one point they missed their way and had to retrace their steps over some fifteen punishing miles of the desolate wasteland. Back on the trail, they passed one derelict prairie schooner after another until, she says, "we seemed to be but the last, feeble, struggling band at the rear of a routed army." At last they reached the Sierras and were escorted over the mountains into California by men of the relief company maintained by the government to assist travelers.

Although the Royces were in search of business opportunities rather than gold, they went through experiences typical of the gold rush, and Josiah Royce quite properly dedicated his book of history: "To My Mother, a California Pioneer of 1849."

Some who set out to be argonauts either died in the attempt or, defeated by the hardships west of the Missouri, turned back. The rest kept going, drawn irresistibly by their golden vision, inspired by the theme song of the trek:

There's plenty of gold,
So I've been told,
On the banks of the Sacramento!

Those who crossed the Sierras came down directly into the gold regions of California. Those who came by sea landed at San Francisco and proceeded to their destinations by way of the Sacramento River or else along the trails that grew wider every day from the tramp of thousands of feet. The argonauts kept coming from both directions, east and west, and from all points of the compass. Americans, Mexicans, Peruvians, Hawaiians, Englishmen, Irishmen, Scots, Frenchmen, Germans, Russians, South Africans,

Australians, Chinese, Hindus—they poured into California in an eager, excited, avaricious horde and threw themselves like predators on the gold-bearing streams of the Sacramento and San Joaquin valleys.

Gold, and so much of it, happened to be in this part of California because the Sierras form a massive granitic uplift 400 miles long created during the mountain-building process that convulsed the area for eons, most recently about 5 million years ago. Molten gold ran into the crevices of the granite and rose to the surface with it in hardened seams.

Less than 1 million years ago, a titanic fault snapped far underground. The fault dropped Nevada's Owens Valley straight down, sheared off the steep escarpment of the eastern Sierras, and tossed the granite blocks of the western Sierras around like playthings. Volcanic activity covered the tops and slopes of the mountains, but to so shallow a degree that weathering uncovered gold seams along whole tracts of the Sierras. Erosion loosened fragments of ore and tumbled them down into the foothills. Gold—dust, flakes, or nuggets—fell into the streams to be carried along until stopped by sandbars, rapids, or other obstructions.

Much of California's Great Valley constituted a series of goldfields where the metal could be retrieved from rocks with a knife, from the ground with a shovel, from the water with a pan, and often by simply picking it up where it lay loose and unencumbered.

The primary source, the famed Mother Lode, extended for over 100 miles with the greatest gold concentration between the Yuba River in the north and the Merced River in the south. Gold lay so profusely in the foothills of the Sierras that miners speculated about the ultimate source being a solid gold mountain up in the summits of the chain, and some loaded their burros with picks and shovels and went looking for it. These prospectors may have used the cliché so beloved of Hollywood producers of grade-B movies: "There's gold in them thar hills!"

Isaac Humphrey, from Georgia, who learned gold mining in his native state, was the first to pan for gold in 1848. Hearing in San Francisco about Sutter's mill and identifying the products of the millrace as gold, Humphrey went to Coloma and panned the South Fork of the American River.

Employing this most simple of methods, he took a pan with low, slanted sides, dredged up sand and gravel from the riverbed, and sloshed the contents around and around in a circular motion. The lighter debris slid over the side, the heavier remained in the pan. That was how Isaac Humphrey took his first gold from the South Fork.

Then he built a cradle, or rocker, of a conventional type already known among miners and destined for a long future in the Mother Lode country. This was a wooden box on

This picture (opposite) captures the essence of the typical gold miner.

Cradles (gravel-washing machines), pans, and gravel buckets used in placer mining are shown in this 1850 daguerreotype.

A sluice fed by water could handle up to 100 cubic yards of gravel a day if the miners could shovel it that fast.

rockers holding a hopper pierced with holes through which water-soaked sand and gravel could leak down into the bottom of the box. Humphrey poured water over the debris in the hopper while rocking the cradle, a movement that brought the debris over the holes. What filtered through ran out the other end of the box where a series of flat horizontal bars, or riffles, allowed the water to pass but stopped the gold. Humphrey found gold in the South Fork with this equipment, too.

Most miners used pan or cradle. Later came the long tom, based on the same principle as the cradle, an inclined plane ending in an upturned end riddled with holes. Water containing earthy debris ran down the plane, seeped through the holes, and again kept going while the gold remained caught behind the riffles.

The point about the long tom was that it could handle more material than the cradle and keep several men busy at the same time. The sluice went farther in this direction by using a series of riffle boxes placed end to end. A large number of men could work the sluice together, some digging up the earth, others shoveling it in, still others transporting the needed water. Big operations developed from this method. Companies formed, enormous sluices were built, and streams were diverted through ditches and flumes to maintain a constant flow of water.

Where gold lay in the cliffs, miners might get to it by tunneling. An easier and more effective method was hydraulic mining. A hose and a powerful jet of water cut into hillsides so that water and earth were mixed together as they coursed down the hill, the water going where it would, the gold lodging behind the stones and other natural "rifflles."

The Middle Fork of the American River turned out to be the richest of the Great Valley streams that surrendered gold to the men who panned their water or delved into their banks. Edward Gould Buffum says in his journal that he traveled the Middle Fork for thirty miles on both sides and every time he washed a pan, he found gold. He judged that 10,000 miners were at work along this tributary at the height of the gold fever, almost literally a fever because of the continual agitation in the minds of those who were searching and hoping.

Buffum has a personal description of what it felt like to strike gold. He had dug into the earth and found a crevice in a large rock: "It appeared to be filled with a hard bluish clay and gravel, which I took out with my knife, and there at the bottom, strewn along the whole length of the rock, was bright yellow gold, in little pieces about the size and shape of a grain of barley. Eureka! Oh how my heart beat! I sat still and looked at it some minutes before I touched it, greedily drinking in the pleasure of gazing upon gold that was in my

Overleaf: This beautiful Currier and Ives depicts many aspects of gold mining.

49

These six poses of gold-rush men and women have a rogues'-gallery quality. The women are particularly grim.

very grasp, and feeling a sort of independent bravado in allowing it to remain there."

Such was the great moment every argonaut prayed for. The shout of "Color!" galvanized everyone within earshot. It might mean a few flakes of gold and nothing more; or a moderate haul of small nuggets; or a strike substantial enough to make the finder a rich man. The largest single nugget, weighing 195 pounds, was taken from Carson Hill.

While hard work led to discoveries, so did pure chance. One miner is said to have pulled up a plant and found gold dust clinging to the roots. Another is said to have stumbled over a rock, kicked it angrily, and noticed as it rolled over that it contained gold. Lady Luck ruled in the goldfields, and no one knew it better than the men who lived and labored there.

These men came from all kinds of backgrounds, for gold is, in its enticement, no respecter of persons. New Helvetia lost farmers, storekeepers, blacksmiths, soldiers, and servants at the beginning of the gold rush, and the same types and many more kept coming in from all over. Sailors of a dozen nations jumped ship in San Francisco Bay to search for gold. No class was immune to the gold fever, not clergymen, or professors, or judges. Bayard Taylor, himself a scholar, commented that he "met daily with men of education and intelligence."

For a while after arriving, these varied miners dressed and looked like individuals. After a year or so in the diggings, they began to conform to a nondescript pattern. There being few women around, the miners went unshaven and allowed their hair to grow long and unkempt. They wore a common costume put together from what they could buy in the stores or from traveling salesmen—flannel shirt, slouch hat, battered boots, and rough trousers. A Jewish draper from Germany, Levi Strauss, carried bolts of cloth around the Horn and introduced trousers so practical in the mines and elsewhere that they became permanent additions to America's outdoor dress. We still know them by the name Strauss gave them—levis.

Laboring under a California sun, constantly dousing themselves with water, sleeping as they could, often on the ground under dirty blankets, the miners quickly acquired a variety of aches and pains. Meals were the kind to cause dyspepsia, especially the flapjacks and pickled pork that were standard until fresh food began arriving from California farms.

For some miners, California was a round of suffering ending in despair. Hiram Pierce of Troy, New York, found so little gold that he ran into debt, gave up, headed for home by way of Panama, and died of malaria contracted on the isthmus. He was not the only one who left. Leeper noted that each of the main goldfields was a two-way street where the hopeful traveled in one direction, the despairing in the other: "And thus we found it everywhere—some coming, some going; some praising, some damning."

Psychological problems often afflicted those who failed to strike it rich. Men afraid to go home and confess their failure in California took obscure jobs or became derelicts haunting saloons and brothels. Pathetic inquiring letters from anxious women—wives and fiancées waiting at home to be sent for—went unanswered, frequently because the addressee could not be located.

Miners who wanted to create difficulties for anyone on their tracks did so by adopting assumed names, something they could get away with because practically no one ever became inquisitive. A miner working his claim seldom knew who the stranger on another claim 100 yards away might be. When they met, there would be no questions about why either was there, and for all either knew, the other fellow might be an absconding embezzler from New York or a murderer from Chicago on the run from the police.

The right to anonymity was part of the unwritten code of the mining camps and was respected as faithfully as in the French Foreign Legion.

Many an individual went by a mere nickname. Bayard Taylor never asked the name or the home of the character

Crowds (opposite, top), anxiously waiting for mail and news from home, line up at the San Francisco post office.

Abandoned ships (opposite, bottom) were sometimes run aground, high and dry, to become instant stores and hotels in booming San Francisco.

who interested him and whom he knew simply as "Buckshot." This man was a gourmet who took sufficient gold from his claim to subsidize an inordinate taste for fine foods, especially oysters and champagne, which cost him a small fortune. He was willing, able, and anxious to pay for a bottle of champagne that began its travels in France, came ashore in San Francisco, and rode the stagecoach from his victualer's emporium to his mining camp. He dug for gold until he had enough to pay for a shipment of the best comestibles, knocked off long enough to devour them, and then repeated the process. He made over $30,000 and spent it all in this manner, according to Taylor. He must have been the most engaging eccentric of the gold rush.

Miners came and went for personal reasons, but the mining camps went on until the gold petered out.

Coloma, where it all started, continued for some time to be a place where rich strikes were possible. New mining camps were founded by indivduals who, after seeing its auriferous rocks and soil, recognized the same formations elsewhere and began digging into them. They, too, stimulated imitators. Like a stone hitting a pond, a gold strike would send ripples outward. Like the ripples rebounding from the shore back into the pond, miners would congregate all around the strike to see if the treasure extended widely enough to be interesting.

Miners in naming their camps could be literal—Placerville, Grass Valley—or sardonic, as in the cases of Dead Man's Hollow, Drunkard's Bar, Delirium Tremens, Hell's Half Acre, Rat Trap Slide. Bret Harte exploited the rowdy vocabulary of the goldfields in "The Luck of Roaring Camp" and "The Outcasts of Poker Flat."

A camp generally began with a few men living out in the open or in a rough lean-to and evolved into a small town of wooden houses. The saloon often was the first building in the camp, for mining was a trade at which a man could work up a parching thirst, and those in from their claims would gather where the hard liquor was. After the saloon came the gambling den in which they could find excitement and perhaps rake in more gold than in the diggings or, often, lose all they had. A hotel, general store, and residence for those called, euphemistically, "dance hall girls," all were part of mining camp life where it flourished for any length of time. Eventually the professions would be represented. Schools and churches would be built, or at least rooms would be used for classes and services, as men brought their families and a more orderly life began.

The places favorably situated for trade, commerce, and farming evolved into cities, led by Stockton on the San Joaquin and, particularly, by Sacramento, which replaced New Helvetia.

Sutter was ruined by the gold rush. Miners overran his estate, devoured his crops, smashed his fences, broke into his storehouses, and killed his livestock. His sawmill failed shortly after it went into operation as incomers settled like locusts on the Coloma region. Even if his property had remained unmolested, he still would have failed because no hired hands could be found who would work for wages when gold was to be had for the taking.

Sutter should have become rich himself from the diggings, but he lacked the character to switch from the pleasant life of his barony to prospecting for gold. The strangers closing in on him drove him to drink. In his forays into the goldfields, he took big parties to do the work, whose members went off to dig for themselves.

His debts overtook him. By 1852 he was bankrupt, and the remainder of his life turned into a nightmare of disappointments as he strove fruitlessly to persuade the courts and the U.S. Government that one Mexican land grant should be restored to him or that he should be granted a pension. California did provide him with a small pension, but he was nearly destitute when he died in 1880.

The end of New Helvetia came when Sutter's son sold lots for a town to be called "Sacramento," which expanded over the area of Sutter's Fort and along the confluence of the Sacramento and American rivers. The town's situation in the heart of the Great Valley, in the middle of river systems joining north and south, brought it prosperity and a lofty future in the history of California when it became the state capital in 1854.

James Marshall profited from the gold rush no more than did Sutter. Marshall suffered from a personality problem. He was an injustice collector who preferred to fail in his prospecting, then complain thereafter with self-righteous indignation that he, the discoverer to whom all the successful gold seekers owed everything, never made anything out of his discovery. He also took to drink, and when his wits were befuddled by liquor, he would recount his doleful tale since the moment he saw gold in the millrace at Sutter's sawmill. When sober, he made some money writing and lecturing on the subject. After his death in 1885, California erected a monument to him at Coloma.

When the misfortunes of Sutter and Marshall began in earnest in 1849 and became increasingly worse during the next few years, the miners responsible knew nothing about it and cared less. They were too busy staking claims and establishing mining camps to wonder who had been there before they arrived.

The camps were international communities and are now of special interest to historians and philosophers for that reason. The miners offered an example of men of different nationalities converging on a single spot and starting a community from the ground up. Anarchy was the last thing a mining camp could stand, and therefore to introduce a modicum of social order ranked high among its needs. The American administrators and generals on the coast had their hands full transforming a Mexican province into a state of the Union (statehood came in 1850), and they lacked the men to enforce the laws in the camps in the Great Valley. The miners had to make do for themselves.

They did very well, all things considered. It was a tribute to American democracy, for the Americans were naturally the dominant group. They took the lead by resorting to forms they were familiar with—voting, majority rule, election of officials and magistrates. The rules and regimes often would have appalled a New England town meeting or a Philadelphia lawyer, but they worked in the hurly-burly of the multinational California goldfields.

With so wild an influx over so much territory, the first problem of every community was to decide who owned what among men who hurried into the goldfields, established themselves in open spaces, and made "claims" to their areas in different languages. The second problem was to sort out the claims and to settle disputes between two or more claimants to the same spot. Each mining camp acted on its own according to circumstances, but one pattern was generally accepted.

J. M. Hutchings did poorly as a miner, but he successfully printed and sold 100,000 copies of "The Miner's Ten Commandments" (opposite), originally created as a joke.

58

No. I.

No. VII.

No. II.

THE MINER'S TEN COMMANDMENTS.

A man spake these words and said: I am a miner, who wandered "from away down east," and came to sojourn in a strange land and "see the elephant." And behold I saw him, and bear witness, that from the key of his trunk to the end of his tail, his whole body has passed before me; and I followed him until his huge feet stood still before a clapboard shanty; then, with his trunk extended, he pointed to a candle-card tacked upon a shingle, as though he would say read, and I read the

Miners' Ten Commandments.

I.

Thou shalt have no other claim than one.

II.

Thou shalt not make unto thyself any false claim, nor any likeness to a mean man, by jumping one; whatever thou findest on the top above, or on the rock beneath, or in a crevice underneath the rock—or I will visit the miners around to invite them on my side; and when they decide against thee, thou shalt take thy pick and thy pan, thy shovel, and thy blankets, with all that thou hast, and "go prospecting," to seek good diggings; but thou shalt find none. Then, when thou findest returned, in sorrow shalt thou find that thine old claim is worked out, and yet no pile made thee, to hide in the ground, or in an old boot beneath thy bunk, or in buckskin or bottle underneath thy cabin, but hast paid all that was in thy purse away, worn out thy boots and thy garments, so that there is nothing good about them but the pockets, and thy patience is likened unto thy garments; and at last thou shalt hire thy body out to make thy board and save thy bacon.

III.

Thou shalt not go prospecting before thy claim gives out. Neither shalt thou take thy money, nor thy gold dust, nor thy good name, to the gaming table in vain; for monte, twenty-one, roulette, faro, lansquenet and poker, will prove to thee that the more thou put test down the less thou shalt take up; and when thou thinkest of thy wife and children, thou shalt not hold thyself guiltless, but—insane.

IV.

Thou shalt not remember what thy friends do at home on the Sabbath day, lest the remembrance may not compare favorably with what thou doest here. Six days thou mayest dig or pick all that thy body can stand under; yet thou washest all thy dirty shirts, darnest all thy stockings, tap thy boots, mend thy clothing, chop thy whole week's firewood, make up and bake thy bread and boil thy pork and beans, that thou wait not when thou returnest from thy long-tom, weary. For in six days' labor only thou canst not work enough to wear out thy body in two years; but if thou workest hard on Sunday also, thou canst do it in six months; and thou, and thy son, and thy daughter, thy male friend and thy female friend, try morals and thy conscience, be none the be for thee for it; but reproach thee, shouldst thou ever return with thy worn-out body to thy mother's fireside; and thou strive to justify thyself, because the trader and the blacksmith, the carpenter and the merchant, the tailors, Jews, and buccaneers, defy God and civilization, by keeping not the Sabbath day, nor wish for a day of rest, such as memory, youth and home, made hallowed.

V.

Thou shalt not think more of all thy gold, and how thou canst make it fastest, than how thou wilt enjoy it, after thou hast ridden, rough shod, over thy good old parent's precepts and examples, that thou mayest have nothing to reproach and sting thee, when thou art left ALONE in the land where thy father's blessing and thy mother's love hath sent thee.

VI.

Thou shalt not kill thy body by working in the rain, even though thou shalt make enough to buy physic and attendance with. Neither shalt thou kill thy neighbor's body in a duel; for, by "keeping cool," thou canst save his life and thy conscience. Neither shalt thou destroy thyself by getting "tight," nor "slewed," nor "high," nor "corned," nor "half-seas-over," nor "three sheets in the wind," by drinking smoothly down—"brandy-slings," "gin-cocktails," "whisky-punches," "rum-toddies," nor "egg-nogs." Neither shalt thou suck "mint-juleps," nor "sherry-cobblers," through a straw, nor gurgle from a bottle the "raw material," nor "take it neat" from a decanter, for, while thou art swallowing down thy purse, and thy coat from off thy back, thou art burning the coat from off thy stomach; and, if thou couldst see the houses and lands, and gold dust, and home comforts already lying there—"a huge pile"—thou shouldst feel a choaking in thy throat; and when to that, thou addest thy crooked walkings and hiccuping talkings, of lodgings in the gutter, or of boilings in the sun, of prospect holes half full of water, and of shafts and ditches, from which thou hast emerged like a drowning rat, thou wilt feel disgusted with thyself, and inquire "Is thy servant a dog, that he doeth these things?" verily I will say, Farewell, old bottle, I will kiss thy gurgling lips no more. And thou, slings, cocktails, punches, smashes, cobblers, nogs, toddies, sangarees, and juleps, forever farewell. Thy remembrance shames me, henceforth, I "cut thy acquaintance," and headaches, tremblings, heart burnings, blue-devils, and all the unholy catalogue of evils that follow in thy train. My wife's smiles and my children's merry-hearted laugh, shall charm and reward me for having the manly firmness and courage to say NO. I wish thee an eternal farewell.

VII.

Thou shalt not grow discouraged, nor think of going home before thou hast made thy "pile," because thou hast not "struck a lead," nor found a "rich crevice," nor sunk a hole upon a "pocket," lest in going home thou shalt leave four dollars a day, and go to work, ashamed, at fifty cents, and serve thee right; for thou knowest by staying here, thou mightest strike a lead and fifty dollars a day, and keep thy manly self-respect, and then go home with enough to make thyself and others happy.

VIII.

Thou shalt not steal a pick, or a shovel, or a pan, from thy fellow miner; nor take away his tools without his leave; nor borrow those he cannot spare; nor return them broken, nor trouble him to fetch them back again; nor talk with him while his water rent is running on; nor remove his stake to enlarge thy claim, nor undermine his bank in following a lead, nor pan out gold from his "riffle-box," nor wash the "tailings" from his sluice's mouth. Neither shalt thou pick out specimens from the company's pan to put them in thy mouth, or in thy purse; nor cheat thy partner of his share; nor steal from thy cabin-mate his gold dust, to add to thine, for he will be sure to discover what thou hast done, and will straightway call his fellow miners together, and if the law hinder them not, they will hang thee, or give thee fifty lashes, or shave thy head and brand thee, like a horse thief, with R upon thy cheek, to be known and read of all men, Californians in particular.

IX.

Thou shalt not tell any false tales about "good diggings in the mountains" to thy neighbor, that thou mayest benefit a friend who hath mules, and provisions, and tools, and blankets, he cannot sell—lest in deceiving thy neighbor, when he returneth through the snow, with naught save his rifle, he present thee with the contents thereof, and like a dog, thou shalt fall down and die.

X.

Thou shalt not commit unsuitable matrimony, nor covet "single blessedness"; nor forget absent maidens; nor neglect thy "first love";—but thou shalt consider how faithfully and patiently she awaiteth thy return; yea, and covereth each epistle that thou sendest with kisses of kindly welcome—until she hath thyself. Neither shalt thou covet thy neighbor's wife, nor trifle with the affections of his daughter; yet, if thy heart be free, and thou love and covet each other, thou shalt "pop the question" like a man, lest another more manly than thou art, should step in before thee, and thou love her in vain, and in the anguish of thy heart's disappointment, thou shalt quote the language of the great, and say, "sich is life"; and thy future lot be that of a poor, lonely, despised and comfortless bachelor.

A new Commandment give I unto thee—if thou hast a wife and little ones, that thou lovest dearer than thy life—that thou keep them continually before thee, to cheer and urge thee onward until thou canst say, "I have enough—God bless them—I will return." Then as thou journiest towards thy much loved home, with open arms shall they come forth to welcome thee, and falling upon thy neck, weep tears of unutterable joy that thou art come; then in the fullness of thy heart's gratitude, thou shalt kneel before thy Heavenly Father together, to thank Him for thy safe return. AMEN—so mote it be!

FORTY-NINE.

No. VIII.

No. III.

No. IV.

No. V.   SUN PRINT, SAN FRANCISCO.   **No. VI.**

No. IX.

No. X.

Chinese laborers in the thousands came to work the mines. Widespread prejudice of citizen-miners made life miserable for the Chinese and other foreign prospectors, as well as for Mexican-Americans and Indians.

When enough miners occupied an area, the Americans summoned an organizational meeting at which part of the group frequently had to be addressed in sign language. The French were called "Keskydees" because, when the English meaning escaped them, they had a habit of asking one another: "*Qu'est-ce qu'il dit?*" ("What did he say?")

The organizational meeting decreed that majority rule

would settle ordinary issues. The miners elected a recorder to keep a register of mining claims and named a group to serve as a jury to settle disputes. They adopted laws stating that the discoverer held title to his claim, that he must be on the site and show signs of working it to justify continuance of his title (no absentee landlords in the goldfields), and that he had a right to twice as much land as those who moved into the area later. The size allotted to each claim in the vicinity of the mining camp depended on the nature of the terrain.

Since claim jumping did occur, especially where the claims were isolated or distant from the camp, and since gold naturally bred the crimes associated with it from the beginning of time—robbery, fraud, murder—the miners devised a system of justice. Sometimes they elected a sheriff or a vigilance committee. Both of these institutions flourished in the West after the gold rush was over. Sometimes miners held special meetings to act as a jury of the whole with power to inflict banishment, flogging, or hanging. The right of lynch mobs to make summary judgments and execute them at once was a recognized, if not particularly legal, method of dealing with criminals.

The most celebrated criminal in miner folklore was Joaquin Murieta, described as a native Californian who, purportedly in retaliation for being abused and victimized by some Americans, turned outlaw and terrorized the Mother Lode country until he was shot to death by a posse. "Rattlesnake Dick" was a failed miner who became a successful highwayman and died with his boots on.

"Irish Dick" killed a man in a quarrel in a gambling den and did it in so atrocious a manner that a band of horrified witnesses hustled him out to the nearest tree. They had the grace to allow him some last words, thinking that the reprobate might confess his wickedness or say a prayer before being sent on his way into the next world. Instead, Irish Dick cooly pulled a deck of cards from his pocket and shuffled them with his customary aplomb and skill. "If anybody wants to buck," he said in the gambling vernacular, "I'll give him a layout."—he would deal to anyone to wanted to play. Incensed, his listeners soon had him dangling at the end of a rope.

One crime rarely punished was the violence committed by white miners against nonwhites. The Americans carried their prejudices with them. They disliked all foreigners, but they managed to give most Europeans a tolerably fair shake. The Hispanic Californians presented a problem since it was difficult to see how they could be considered foreigners. They were, nonetheless, subjected to insulting discrimination and suffered violence at the hands of white men. The Chinese had a worse time, for they were considered strange, sinister creatures slinking around and stealing American

This portrait shows Joaquin Murieta, legendary bandit, standing defiantly in front of a poster offering a reward for his capture, dead or alive.

61

gold—a peculiarly outrageous perversion of the truth, which was that the Chinese tried to stay out of the way by picking over claims that white men had exploited and abandoned. Some Chinese abandoned the search for gold and started two American institutions—the Chinese laundry and the Chinese restaurant. The worst treatment of all was meted out to the original inhabitants of the Sierras, the Indians, who not only were driven away from gold strikes they made but were liable to be shot on sight.

Although violent racism may have motivated only a minority of Americans and although a smaller minority protested openly, it remains the ugliest side of the gold rush.

A better side of the gold rush was the generosity of the miners to those down on their luck. Typically, a collection would be taken to pay a loser's passage home or to help his family until he could get back on his feet. The miners were chivalrous toward respectable women, a fact to which Sarah Royce testified. They became sentimental over children, for instance, over little Lotta Crabtree.

As a small child, Lotta Crabtree revealed a native talent for singing, dancing, emoting, and acting. She lived with her parents in various mining camps, for her father cherished the eternal hope of the miner that tomorrow, or next week, he would strike gold. He moved the family around while he staked unproductive claims, and ended up empty-handed. He never realized that he had a fortune at home in his daughter.

Lotta entertained guests with winsome or impish performances, singing sad ballads, reciting comic verse, and charming everyone who saw her. One of the latter was the celebrated Lola Montez, who, having ended her quasi-official reign in Bavaria as the friend of King Ludwig I—she "abdicated" by popular request of the Bavarian people—took her new, voluptuous, erotic style of dancing around Europe and America.

She seems to have had a penchant for gold and miners, and we will meet her again in the Australian goldfields. The mining camps of California offered her a chance to display her art because theaters, often merely tents or cleared barroom floors, catered to the miners' taste for theatrical performances. Individuals and companies from San Francisco and other cities, and some local talent, toured these theaters where patrons balanced gold dust on a scale to buy a ticket and where a satisfied audience might rain nuggets onto the stage.

All of this suited Lola Montez, who in 1853 arrived in Grass Valley, a mining camp near the Yuba River. She of course made a splash, as she always did, and soon she knew practically everybody in Grass Valley, including the Crabtree family.

Lotta Crabtree (opposite) was coached as a child by the notorious Lola Montez (below). Lotta, who had talent, grew up to become America's top comedienne. Both women are shown smoking, something not socially acceptable at the time.

San Francisco in 1847 — from the hill back.

James Marshall's face reflects the disappointments he suffered. While he found the first nugget, gold did not stick to his fingers and he lived his last years in abject poverty.

After seeing Lotta's naive performances, Lola judged that the child was so gifted as to be worth tutoring professionally. Lessons began with the approval of Lotta's mother, and Lola taught her pupil soft-shoe dancing, light-comedy techniques, and how to time the reaction of an audience. (Thoughtfully excluded from these rehearsals was the "Spider Dance" with which Lola scandalized audiences from Munich to San Francisco.)

Lotta justified Lola's faith in her. She appeared in mining-camp theaters, enchanted the rough men from the goldfields, and used winsome tricks such as pretending not to know what the nuggets were that landed at her feet. In a few years she was appearing with professional troupes, and then she branched out on her own into the wider theater world of San Francisco. From there she went to New York and London, became an international star, and reigned as a queen of light comedy until her retirement in 1891.

Lotta Crabtree never forgot her origins or how her acting career had been launched. Among the donations she made from her vast wealth was a fountain for San Francisco. The city at the Golden Gate had changed beyond recognition over the years. In 1848 it was a sleepy coastal village largely Hispanic in population. The forty-niners transformed it into a boomtown, and from there it developed into the plush Americanized metropolis of the 1850s and after, famous for Nob Hill, Chinatown, and the Barbary Coast.

While San Francisco, Sacramento, and Stockton boomed, towns like Placerville and Grass Valley declined. Built on gold, they could not maintain their prosperity when gold was no longer easy to come by, when the streams were panned out and the shallow earth stripped of its ore. The precious metal taken from the goldfields during the decade after the discovery amounted to over $500 million, with 1852 the peak year at $80 million, but the inevitable decline set in after that.

Although it is impossible to say precisely when the gold rush ended, the stupendous mass movement of men from the ends of the earth to California was over by 1853. Those intoxicated by the gold fever had already come, and those who had stayed behind lacked the intense passion that inspires crusades, pilgrimages—and gold rushes.

The era of hope for large gold strikes by ordinary men using elementary equipment was over by 1859. Productive prospecting required technicians with machines, and placer miners, their occupation gone, kept slipping away. California's mining camps became ghost towns. This drift received an impetus in the decennial year of the gold rush by two bonanzas east of California.

The Comstock Lode caused a rush eastward over the Sierras into Nevada. Here George Hearst laid the basis of

Placerville, earlier known as Old Dry Diggings and as Hangtown, because of the illegal hanging of three men, was a hodge-podge of log-and-lumber buildings, a typical sprawling, disorganized mining town.

the Hearst fortune that enabled his son, William Randolph, to found a chain of newspapers and to build and furnish his castle at San Simeon, California. A journalist named Mark Twain made a name for himself by contributing articles to the Virginia City *Territorial Enterprise*.

The bonanza in the Rockies produced a rush into those mountains and added a slogan to the American language: "Pike's Peak or Bust!" In 1878 the Homestake Mine in South Dakota began surrendering its huge cache of gold, and in 1891 came the discovery of gold in Cripple Creek, Colorado, an area that knew young men who would become famous for other reasons—Jack Dempsey, Groucho Marx, Lowell Thomas.

And yet none of these places ever had the romance, the drama, the energy, the sheer high spirits, of the gold rush of forty-nine. Long after the dispersal of the hordes of miners who had flocked to the Sacramento and San Joaquin rivers and their tributaries, long after silence had fallen over the areas that once had heard the slosh of the mining pan and the thud of the miner's ax, thousands of men relived in memory and talk the greatest experience of their lives:

The days of old, the days of gold,
The days of forty-nine.

Chapter Three
The Fossickers

The jaunty Australians have contributed racy and expressive words to the international lingo we call the English language—*swagman* and *billabong* will occur to anyone who has heard that immortal anthem from Down Under, "Waltzing Matilda"—and one such term appears in the title of this chapter. The verb *to fossick* means in the Australian vernacular to hunt or to rummage, and more particularly it signifies to glean in a gold area that has already been harvested. Fossickers are therefore gold seekers in the land of the kangaroo and platypus.

All of which implies that the Australians had a gold rush of their own, and so they did, one of the richest in the history of mining. It started, coincidentally, in 1851, while California's gold rush was still in full swing.

The Australian gold rush might have begun nearly thirty years earlier, for in 1823 a surveyor named James McBrian reported finding bits of the precious metal in the hills near Bathurst, New South Wales. The McBrian report produced no effect at the time for several reasons.

The gold was so small in size and quantity that McBrian considered mining it uneconomical, hardly worth the time and energy. If a surveyor felt that way, those who knew about his discovery were not likely to make a dash for the hills to endure the hardships of retrieving paltry amounts.

Secondly, under the law all minerals on public lands belonged to the Crown, that is, to His Majesty King George IV. Should real treasure be discovered, the "lucky" man would have to stand aside while the governor of the colony, acting on orders from London, shipped it out or put it to work in the interest of his administration. The possibility of personal gain for a prospector did not exist, and without it there could be no gold rush in Australia or anywhere else.

Thirdly, the colonial government concealed McBrian's report, and others that reached Sydney from time to time, for fear of the consequences if the convicts of Australia absconded to search for gold.

The transportation to Australia of undesirables from the British Isles, which began in 1788 when 716 convicted felons landed at Botany Bay, was still in force in 1823 (it would not end completely until 1860). Many overcrowded British prisons were emptied of desperate criminals, political offenders, or thousands who had been found guilty of smaller crimes such as poaching and sheep stealing. Herded aboard ship, the convicts took the long voyage to Australia where, safely remote from Great Britain, they could not easily return and could be put to useful work in a society very short of labor.

The most obdurate of these forced immigrants slaved in penal colonies. The corrigible worked for the government on public projects like laying roads and erecting administrative buildings. Those considered trustworthy often entered private service as farmhands or domestic help on the estates of free immigrants who came to Australia to make new lives for themselves.

The convicts played a central role in building the colony because, apart from their work, they created a demand for food, clothing, and shelter that boosted the economy. Moreover, those who served their sentences usually settled down as law-abiding members of society.

In throwing a veil of silence over the gold discoveries of 1823 and after, the colonial government wanted to prevent a stampede away from ordinary jobs and the resultant paralysis of life in Sydney. The fear existed, furthermore, that convicts would pour into the goldfields, establish criminal communities, and create a problem that might prove too much for the authorities to handle. Australia had seemed a place where convicts would serve out their sentences without hope of escape. Who could say what would happen if they suddenly found themselves in possession of sufficient gold to bribe officials to let them out and to pay sea captains to take them home to England?

Discovery of gold in 1851 brought different results. News of the successful California gold rush generated a bad case of gold fever in Australia. Gold was discovered in Australia in formations similar to those of California, creating the hope of a comparable bonanza. And the discoverer trumpeted the news to all and sundry.

Edward Hargraves made a direct connection between California and Australia. English by birth, Australian by adoption, Hargraves had been a grazier and an innkeeper before he joined the rush from Down Under to the American territory on the West Coast.

Chinese laborers are "off to the diggings" in this 1856 lithograph.

In the California Great Valley, Hargraves and some companions prospected without any great results. As he worked on his claim, he found a new idea germinating in his mind. Watching how gold was panned from the streams and dug from the hills, he was struck by the resemblance of the auriferous rock to geological formations he had seen back home. If California granite held gold, why not Australian granite?

The thought teased his mind until Hargraves, a failure in California, determined to go back and find the answer to his question. The promising region he had noticed lay to the west of Sydney across the Blue Mountains. Returning to the capital of New South Wales, he set out on horseback across the mountains by way of Parramatta and Penrith to Bathurst. At Guyong the son of the widow Lister, the local innkeeper, joined him, and the pair rode on into the area of the Macquarie River.

*Two miners discuss the prospects
of finding gold on their diggings.*

Choosing a tributary with his California experience in mind, Hargraves on February 12, 1851, panned the gold that convinced him a goldfield lay all around in the stream and the hills. According to his memoirs, he shouted gleefully to his companion: "This is a memorable day in the history of New South Wales! I shall be a baronet, you will be knighted, and my old horse will be stuffed, put into a glass case, and sent to the British Museum!"

None of these things happened, but Hargraves did start Australia's gold rush. After riding around the area and finding more gold, he returned to Sydney and announced his discovery to the colonial secretary. The government sent its surveyor to check, the report was affirmative, and Hargraves received a £500 reward and appointment to the post of Commissioner of Crown Lands.

This official position gave him everything he wanted. A stout figure with muttonchop whiskers, receding hairline, and jovial expression, accoutered in the latest fashion, down to his kid gloves and top hat, Hargraves attracted the attention he reveled in as he rode from camp to camp in a splendid carriage accompanied by liveried servants and outriders. This was his métier since he had never intended to resume the rough, rugged life of the gold miner.

By the time Hargraves became commissioner, his boast that he would open "an age of gold" had come true. The news of the strike near Bathurst sent crowds streaming out of Sydney and over the Blue Mountains in the first of the spreading waves of the stampede. Clerks, policemen, soldiers, longshoremen, farmers, retired residents of the city, and more dropped whatever they were doing to pursue the golden vision. Sailors jumped ship in Sydney harbor as they had in San Francisco Bay.

The Parramatta Road became a welter of horse-drawn vehicles, men on horseback, and pedestrians. Women and children accompanied some of the men on the move toward Eldorado. Slum dwellers of Sydney took to the road pushing wheelbarrows that contained all their worldly possessions. Even this early in the gold rush, prostitutes were visible, conspicuously plying their trade in tents or under more bucolic conditions by night along the Bathurst Road.

The first wave of prospectors suffered disappointment for the most part. The journey was longer than they had imagined, the hardships greater, and the chances of finding gold slimmer. More than that, the rains of Australia's wet season came, drenching the gold seekers, the raw weather causing illness and death. Many lost heart, gave up, and struggled through deep mud back to Sydney. Hargraves himself, meeting a party of disgruntled failures, had to gallop away to escape the onslaught of those who blamed him for starting the gold rumor that resulted in their disappointment, discomfort, and disasters.

It looked as if Australia's gold rush might peter out before it really started. Then in July an aborigine tending sheep near Bathurst discovered a block of quartz containing a chunk of gold that, extracted, weighed sixty pounds. A newspaper succinctly noted the consequence of this news: "Bathurst is mad again!"

Tents spring up as the discovery of gold at Bathurst changes grazing land into a mining camp.

The goldfields at Bendigo proved to be richer than those at Bathurst.

The stampede resumed, and this time there was no stopping it.

Hargraves called the area of his strike "Ophir," from the Bible, and here the first big Australian goldfield developed. No one could prevent the wild influx of people forcing their way into the region of the Macquarie and its tributaries. At the same time, the mineral wealth still belonged to the Crown. Accepting these two facts, the authorities in Sydney worked out a compromise: Any miner might remain and work his claim as long as he paid for a license. A mounted police force, the troopers of Australian song and story, supervised the issuing and inspection of licenses and kept the peace among the miners, thus obviating any need for the miners to make their own law and administer their own justice.

The diggings in New South Wales remained relatively law-abiding, but the same could not be said of Victoria, where gold was discovered at Ballarat, Mount Alexander, and Bendigo. Melbourne suffered the typical population hemorrhage of any city near a gold strike. As these Victoria strikes turned out to be the richest in Australia, prospectors flooded in from all over the continent and from around the world, including, as in California, a large contingent of Chinese.

Victoria had a convict problem more extreme than that of

New South Wales because the Van Diemen's Land (Tasmania) penal settlements were nearby. Convicts, galvanized by gold, escaped to terrorize the gold camps, to become bushrangers (outlaws), or to prey on the citizens of Melbourne. One observer wrote: "It is confidently reckoned that above three thousand convicts have come over from Van Diemen's Land, to the great annoyance of the colonists here. Scarcely a day passes in which some person or other is not knocked on the head, assaulted, or robbed, and it is by no means safe to be out of doors after dark."

The troopers and the police of Victoria, assigned to keep the peace in the goldfields, had therefore a much harder job than their opposite numbers in New South Wales. Not only did they have to chase violent convicts, but they also had to maintain a license system more severe than elsewhere—thirty shillings a month from each miner, who for this sum, a large one in the economy of the period, acquired the right to dig in a plot of land only twenty-four feet square. In most cases, the gold production did not justify the expense, and it was the licensing system that led to the worst violence of the gold rush.

The Australian goldfields were near enough to the coast to be accessible from cities like Sydney and Melbourne but far enough back in the bush to be uninhabited and therefore wide open for the establishment of brand new communities.

The difference from California lay mainly in the sobering presence of government and law in Australia.

The first men who occupied a site lived out in the open, under hastily constructed lean-tos, or in tents. They staked their claims, panned the first gold, and watched later arrivals come in and take places near them. Pan, cradle, long tom, sluice, and hydraulic mining were all used at various strikes, but water being less plentiful than in California, the miners improvised a system of "dusting" instead of "washing" their pans. They scooped up dry earth rather than wet sand or gravel, performed the standard circular motions, and allowed the lighter content to slip over the edges of the pan while the heavier gold stayed in it.

Shafts were sunk to get at subsurface gold, the equipment for this method being bucket, rope, and windlass for raising the dirt to the surface. Since miners rarely bothered filling in a shaft before they moved on, a digging soon became pitted with deep holes that constituted an obstacle course for anyone crossing the field.

A mining camp developed gradually. Tents came after the worst kind of roughing it, then wooden buildings, and in time all the necessities of community life could be found within easy distance of the mines. Usually a businessman from Sydney or Melbourne would establish a general store as near the center of the field as he could, which often enough, given the closeness of numerous small claims, put him on the edge of the camp. He filled his shelves with all kinds of goods, where a miner could exchange his gold for a pickax, a flannel shirt, a box of biscuits, or a tin of hard candy. Women could find dresses, aprons, baby clothes, and household utensils.

Enterprises of all types were attracted to the mining camps, and the usual hotel, restaurant, and brothel found places for themselves amid the turmoil of the diggings. At Bendigo the line of tents catering to different needs and tastes stretched for several miles. The government made an attempt to regulate the selling of hard liquor, with the inevitable consequence—the illegal "sly grog shop" became a fixture, the most frequented place in the Australian mining camp.

Women were a civilizing influence. Families could be seen mining with pans and cradles, wives and children helping the men in the frantic search for gold, although some women confined themselves to making life more pleasant for their husbands. According to Ellen Clacy, who saw them at Bathurst, women accommodated themselves to mining camp existence: "Sometimes a wife is at first rather a nuisance. Women get scared and frightened, then cross, and commence to 'blow up' at their husbands. But all this railing generally ends in their quietly settling down to this

S. T. Gill's sketches (above and opposite) provided an invaluable record of mining life in and around Bendigo.

rough and primitive style of living, if not without a murmur, at least to all appearance with the determination to laugh and bear it."

A different type of female made many a miner spruce up. Lord Robert Cecil (the future British prime minister), pausing at Ballarat during his peregrinations through the goldfields, "saw a digger in his jumper and working dress walking arm-in-arm with a woman dressed in the most exaggerated finery, with a parasol of blue damask silk that would have seemed gorgeous in Hyde Park. She was a lady . . . known as Lavinia, who had been graciously condescending enough to be the better half of this unhappy digger for a few days in order to rob him of his earnings."

Diggers who took up with temporary "wives" and spent their money wildly on them could not have been all that unhappy. Too many such couples appeared at Bathurst, Ballarat, and Bendigo. Naturally the women transferred their favors elsewhere when the gold was gone, but in the meantime the miners got what they paid for.

Into this rowdy mining-camp society came the unsinkable Lola Montez, fresh from her triumphs in the Sierra goldfields. Australian miners, too, relaxed in theater tents and rickety buildings where they lavished applause and gold on their favorite thespians, abuse and sometimes violence on those who displeased them. Lola knew how to handle a masculine audience, knew her way around mining camps, and accumulated her share of the gold in Australia.

William Craig, a British traveler and miner who was only twenty-two at the time, was much taken with Lola when he caught her act at Bendigo: "One has only to look at her magnificent dark flashing eyes, her willowy form, the traces of former beauty, and her lithe, active movements to see that one is in the presence of a very remarkable woman, and it is not hard to believe that she should have been able to bewitch a king and cost him his throne."

The entire passage in Craig's book shows how quick-witted Lola could be. During her performance in a melodrama, a violent thunderstorm broke out overhead and a bolt of lightning hit the stage. Whereupon Lola commented archly that if this kept up she and her audience would have to find something else to do, "saying with a coquettish shake of her shapely head and a musical laugh, 'You know!' "

Craig was not quite clear what she meant by those two words, but it is doubtful that any other man in the audience missed the point of her bawdy joke.

Some performers did not require a theater or a stage. They were the miners themselves. Germans played woodwind instruments they had brought with them; Italians vocalized from Rossini operas; and Scots caused the unearthly wailing of the bagpipes to float over the goldfield. At Bendigo a

*A song recital takes place in the concert room
of the Charlie Naprir Hotel in Ballarat.*

group of black Americans toured the camp plunking banjos, punching tambourines, and belting out songs with an insistent beat:

Come, gals, let us sing.
Don't you hear the banjo ring, ring, ring!

All races were represented in the mines. The Australians took a more broadminded view of foreigners than did the Americans in California, but even so animosity surfaced again and again when the Chinese arrived. The government of Victoria placed a tax of £10 on each Chinese, which would have been a crushing financial burden if it had not been evaded so frequently, as were other laws aimed at diminishing the number of immigrants from the Celestial Empire.

The Australian "Indians" were the aborigines, the original inhabitants of the continent. The gold rush exercised a terrible fascination for and had a deplorable effect on tribal youth in the vicinity of the mining camps. These aborigines too often gave up their traditional arts and crafts and whatever work they could find with the settlers and hung around the sly grog shops getting drunk on drinks cadged from miners amused by the spectacle. Troopers and government officials were powerless to arrest the tragedy, which ended only when the camps broke up or graduated into being towns in a respectable society.

The impression one gets of the Australian Eldorado compared to the other famous gold rushes is one of overcrowding, especially in the Victoria fields with their extremely small claim limits. Humanity was crowded together cheek-by-jowl to labor in dust, mud, rain, heat of summer, cold of winter. Contagious diseases threatened to spread across the camp if a single individual was stricken; but the very threat caused preventive precautions to be taken. Dysentery became so deadly a menace that the authorities assumed control of the water supply to make sure that what the miners drank was free from contamination.

The everyday operations in any goldfield caused constant accidents that allowed doctors to practice their vocation profitably—setting broken bones, sewing up flesh wounds, removing splinters from fingers and dust from eyes, and handing out doses of medicine for coughs, chills, and fevers.

Camp undertakers disposed of those who died, hurriedly encasing corpses in boxes of rough-hewn boards and transporting the coffins by wheelbarrow to cemeteries in cleared spaces outside the goldfields. Some of the more pathetic casualties of mining life were children who injured themselves handling equipment or falling into abandoned shafts.

Suffering, tragedy, or disappointment, sometimes all three together, drove miners from the goldfields to try their luck and skill in some other line of work. Most, following their dream of sudden wealth, stuck to their pans and cradles, their pickaxes and buckets. The gold was there.

They knew it was just a question of finding it. So many succeeded that in a decade Victoria alone produced over £100 million of the precious metal.

Australia became known for outsize nuggets lying in the soil, so big they received special names—"Sierra Sands," "Lady Hotham," "Welcome Stranger." The giant, taken from Hill End near Bathurst, was the "Holtermann Nugget," weighing over 200 pounds and therefore worth a small fortune. Finds like these made hope spring eternal in numerous breasts that something nearly as good might be unearthed by the next swing of the pickax.

The first half of the decade was the time of greatest prosperity in the mines and in the cities where the miners went on spending sprees. These were the riotous years of the gold rush when incredibly rich strikes lured immigrants to Australia from around the world, an invasion partly made up of veterans of the California gold rush, including, like Hargraves, Australians returning home, hoping to do better Down Under than they had in the Mother Lode.

At the government camp in each goldfield a commissioner supervised the area by means of foot patrols and troopers. Miners could bring their gold to be stacked in the "gold tent," and when the pile became large enough, it went to banks in the city. A period-piece magazine illustration presents the romantic scene of a gold wagon jouncing out of Ballarat with troopers riding along on horseback as an armed guard for the run down to Melbourne.

Human nature is the same everywhere, and the gold wagons needed armed escorts because they were liable to be stopped and rifled by bushrangers, just as American stagecoaches were held up by outlaws in the Old West. The mail coach had to be protected in both places, and solitary travelers went armed.

The Vandemonians, escaped or freed convicts from Van Diemen's Land, became known as "Demons" from the number of violent crimes they committed or were suspected of committing. At Bendigo, when one Demon murdered his partner and tried to flee with their gold, a crowd of miners lynched him, stringing him up on a branch of the nearest tree in the tradition of what the Australians called "Yankee justice." Another ex-convict received a ducking for theft, and it was done so thoroughly that he drowned.

The caches of gold so near at hand tempted "night fossickers" who toured the best strikes in the dark of the moon and made off with the fruits of other men's labors—a dangerous occupation because angry miners often would not wait for the law to arrive when they caught a would-be robber, but might convene a kangaroo court there and then and carry out the sentence on the spot.

The presence of the law naturally curtailed frontier

The Holterman gold nugget weighed 630 pounds and was 4 feet, 4 inches high by 2 feet, 2 inches wide.

justice, despite the occasional lapse into rough-and-ready procedures; but that presence also troubled the miners, who reserved much of their animosity for the police and the troopers.

The guardians of the law also felt the temptations of the time and place. Gold lay all around, but not for them. The prisoners they arrested frequently possessed the gold to offer substantial bribes, a cause of soul-searching by men who saw unsavory characters getting rich while they themselves worked at a difficult, dangerous trade for low wages. Lawmen knew the miners suspected them of collusion when a criminal got away. And they had to pursue and collar ruffians who would shoot or stab them without turning a hair.

Goldfield policemen had to be stern and authoritative, and inevitably some of them added brutality to the list of characteristics. Superintendent Armstrong of Ballarat made himself notorious for the callousness with which he treated miners who violated camp regulations. Cecil accompanied Armstrong in a raid on a sly grog shop: "The culprit's own spade was used to knock his tent down, and his wife actually helped to pull the stakes out of the ground. All the woodwork was piled and a glorious bonfire was made."

Of all the miners' grievances about the police, however, none equaled the necessity to own a mining license and to show it on demand. The fee had to be paid by everyone, the lucky gold hunters and the unlucky alike. While of little concern to the former, it was a heavy drain on those still searching, causing them to evade payment and to mine illegally.

That was the reason for the periodic "license hunts." Gold commissioners requiring the fees to help pay for their administration of the camps, for the police force, and for the troopers who took the gold to the banks, sent their policemen around the claims to find out who had licenses and who did not. A miner had to stop whatever he was doing when challenged, which perhaps would necessitate his clambering out of a deep shaft, producing his license for inspection, and then descending to resume his work after the loss of what could be productive time.

Miners without licenses absented themselves if they learned in advance that a license hunt was on. They flitted around the goldfield in the hope of escaping notice until the police left, officially criminals who considered they were committing no crime.

The license hunts occurred several times a month, a standing annoyance to all miners and a threat to the delinquent. Complaints abounded about police brutality, while the police in turn accused the miners of lying to, and becoming recalcitrant with, officers doing their duty.

As early as 1851 a miners' meeting at Buninyong took up

This is a copy of the unpopular license that fueled the miners' rebellion against the government.

A poster offers a reward for capture of two Eureka rioters.

the question of licenses when the government published a proclamation warning that the documents were about to be printed and the fees collected. Complaints that would be heard repeatedly were aired at this meeting, where individuals argued that the fee was exorbitant; that it was unfair to the members who had spent all their money on equipment and could not reasonably be expected to pay until they had found gold; and that they were being taxed without being consulted—taxation without representation!

The miners agreed to send an appeal to the government in which they avowed an intention to abandon Buninyong rather than pay. Since gold was soon discovered, the appeal came to nothing, but it was a harbinger of the future at Ballarat.

The gold of Ballarat lay for the most part beneath the surface at levels that could be reached only by the bucket, rope, and windlass technique. Deep shafts had to be sunk wherever miners thought they might strike gold, a hit-or-miss operation that was necessarily long and laborious before gold could be brought out, assuming it was there at all. Weeks or months might pass before a miner hit pay dirt or before he accepted the reality that he was never going to hit it on that claim.

Meanwhile, licenses had to be obtained and fees paid, so that all these gold seekers were expected to pay out money before they made a penny from their labor; and no matter how fruitless their labor, they still had to keep on paying. When a shaft produced no gold, the unfortunate miners could do nothing except, if they were persistent enough, start all over again on another spot. Quite a few, unable to stand that prospect, joined successful groups and worked for wages—and blamed the government for their poverty and humiliation.

In 1854 the governor of Victoria, Sir Charles Hotham, noting a large discrepancy between the numbers of miners in the Ballarat goldfields and the number of licenses issued, ordered a license hunt twice a week, which exacerbated the antigovernment feeling among the miners. A situation developed in which a spark would touch off an explosion.

The government supplied the spark after an ex-convict named James Bentley, owner of a hotel at Ballarat, was accused along with his wife and partner, all Vandemonians, of murdering a miner. The magistrates who heard the case found the accused not guilty and released them. A band of miners, infuriated by the judicial decision and charging collusion between the presiding magistrate and the defendants, stormed into the hotel, which they pillaged, vandalized, and burned.

The governor dispatched a military force to the scene and ordered the re-arrest of Bentley, his wife, and his partner;

Government troops storm and overrun the fortified Eureka Stockade.

but the ringleaders of the mob also were picked up and jailed. The miners assembled and constituted themselves the Ballarat Reform League, which made a series of demands—abolition of licenses, freedom to buy land around the mining camp, the right to vote.

Violence erupted. The miners burned their licenses, Commissioner Robert Rede launched another license hunt, the miners defied the police, and the leaders of the resistance were arrested. The miners held a meeting at Eureka, one of the Ballarat goldfields named for the exclamation of the ancient Greek mathematician Archimedes when he thought of the test for pure gold according to its specific gravity. They sent a delegation to Commissioner Rede with a petition for the release of their imprisoned comrades. Rede refused.

The more rebellious of the miners responded by picking up their guns and moving to a strategic point where they used stones and wooden planks to erect a barrier famous in Australian history as the Eureka Stockade.

An international crew manned this impromptu fortress. Their leader, Peter Lalor, came from Ireland. Of his lieutenants, Raffaello Carboni was an Italian, Charles Ross a Canadian, Frederick Vern a German, and C. D. Ferguson an American who had been a prospector in California before the news from halfway around the world drew him to the goldfields of Australia. Carboni and Ferguson left reports of the Eureka Stockade that correspond so closely that the affair can be reconstructed except for unimportant details.

The rebels flew a flag of defiance, the Southern Cross, a silver cross on a blue ground symbolizing the night sky south of the equator. They took an oath: "We swear by the Southern Cross to stand truly by each other and fight to defend our rights and liberties." They manned the barricades and waited.

Commissioner Rede brought in soldiers as well as troopers and dismounted police, and on December 3 he ordered

Photographs by Beaufoy Merlin (above, opposite, and overleaf), taken in the 1870s, capture the activities of the Australian miners.

his men to take the Eureka Stockade. Shooting erupted as they advanced. The soldiers suffered the first casualties, but what followed could scarcely be termed a battle since the attackers burst into the redoubt and overwhelmed the defenders after a melee lasting only about twenty minutes.

Ross was killed. Carboni and Ferguson were taken prisoner. Lalor and Vern escaped. In all, thirty miners and five soldiers died at the Eureka Stockade, while the wounded amounted to perhaps three times that number on each side. There were many more casualties when vindictive troopers invaded the goldfields and picked fights with miners indiscriminately.

The news of the Eureka Stockade shocked Melbourne, where even Governor Hotham admitted that Commissioner Rede had acted hastily in ordering the attack. It was generally agreed that the rebel force would have disintegrated if left alone, so that, given restraint on the part of the authorities, the affair could have been settled without violence, let alone shooting. Most Australians sympathized with the miners, and juries acquitted those tried for treason.

The system of controlling the goldfields had to change after this episode. The rebellious miners received their vindication when the existing regulations, the license and the exorbitant fee attached to it, were canceled, replaced by a document that cost £1 a year, a sum that beggared no one. The government also abolished the hated administrative system, introduced democratic institutions, and gave the vote to every man who held a miner's license. In a nice twist of fate, Peter Lalor, having led and survived the Eureka Stockade uprising, won a seat in the Legislative Council of Ballarat at the first election.

The Eureka Stockade coincided with a watershed in the history of the Australian gold rush. Surface mining declined sharply into the year 1854, leveled out for a couple of years, and then dropped again. Companies equipped for depth digging took over a larger share of mining operations, and miners who had worked on their own looked elsewhere for a livelihood. They went into business in towns that had been mining camps, Ballarat among them. Ex-miners took jobs in Melbourne, Adelaide, Sydney, and smaller cities, worked as farmhands, and "squatted" on lands, which they were allowed to buy under new legislation.

Because of the gold rush, Australia's population tripled in a decade and the population mix changed. Free immigrants now outnumbered convicts. Most of the immigrants came from England, Ireland, Scotland, and Wales, which gave Australia a strongly British and middle-class society. Europeans re-created their culture, one reflection of this being the establishment of universities, museums, and orchestras.

The economic foundations of a great nation were laid. Ranches, spreading across once desolate terrain, found their markets in the older cities and the newer towns. Railroads, answering the transportation demands of passengers and freight handlers, linked together the coast and the inland regions. The railroads led to the rise of an iron industry that produced the material for locomotives and rails. They allowed an enormously expanded production of wheat, which could be shipped to market before spoiling, and to bigger markets created by a bigger population.

Socially, politically, economically, and culturally, modern Australia is a child of an event that began when Edward Hargraves panned gold near Bathurst in 1851, reached its crisis point in 1854, and was dead by 1861. Gold remained to be discovered and mined in other parts of Australia, but the main gold rush was over.

The tumult and the turmoil ended, and the last of the strident voices in the uproar fell silent.

Chapter Four

The Rise of the Randlords

It would have been a nice example of historical coincidence and continuity if the South African gold rush had begun in 1854 just after Pieter Marais discovered gold in the Transvaal, for Marais had learned the prospecting trade in the goldfields of California and completed his education in those of Australia. He had been both a forty-niner and a fossicker when, on October 7, 1853, while camped on the banks of the Crocodile River, he found some "specks" of gold.

Having come upon more of them in the area, he repaired to Potchefstroom, then the capital of the Transvaal, and made known to the authorities that gold lay in the soil of their region of South Africa and that, with their assent and support, he would prospect for it. The upshot of this conference was a remarkable agreement, signed on December 6, of which one clause stated that should Marais uncover a gold mine, and should he give the information to foreigners, the Boer authorities had a right to execute him forthwith. The Boers, a sparse population of Dutch descent living on isolated farms in the South African hinterland, were determined not to have their lives disrupted by gold seekers from the outside.

Marais found more bits of gold in early 1854 in various places, mainly along the river, and if the Boer authorities had followed this up with a resolute search, the decisive strike might have been made. Unfortunately, Marais came back with too little gold to persuade the hardheaded settlers that they should gamble any money on a mere possibility. When they gambled, they preferred a sure thing, and Marais' find was too dubious for their nerves or their pocketbooks.

They repudiated their prospector, who gave up, shook the dust of the Transvaal from his boots, and disappeared from

A biting cartoon gives an unflattering view of South African President Paul Kruger taking gold coins from the British to finance "war expenses" against them.

the story of the most spectacular bonanza of them all.

More gold discoveries were made in subsequent years, each starting a flurry of interest and one, that to the Blyde River in 1874, a minor gold rush; but the real saga of South African gold begins with the discovery of diamonds.

In 1867 the Orange River area gave up its first diamonds, to be quickly followed by the Vaal River. The breakthrough came at a point near the border of the Cape Colony and the Orange Free State where, in 1871, three incredibly rich diamond mines came to light inside an area about three miles across.

The diamond rush became a stampede. One mining camp with a Dutch name of scrambled vowels and consonants unpronounceable by the English tongue developed into the city of Kimberley, renamed for the Duke of Kimberley, Britain's colonial secretary.

Only a few of the precious stones of Kimberley lay on or near the surface where they could be scooped up. The true fortune was hidden underground, and the only way to reach it was to sink cylindrical shafts straight down. The nearly vertical sides of these shafts caused earth slides and rockfalls. As a result, open-pit mining became difficult at a shallow level and impossible at great depths. This put small-time miners out of business since they could not afford the expense of the only digger that would do the trick—heavy machinery. Diamond mining became the preserve of rich, powerful, ruthless, and persuasive men who formed corporations, raised capital in large quantities, and introduced the machines that could bite deep into the earth.

One such man, Cecil Rhodes, the son of a vicar of the Church of England, came from London to South Africa in 1870. Following the diamond strike of 1871, Rhodes and his brother staked a claim and began the exploit the De Beers Mine. Here Rhodes founded the fortune that enabled him to become an empire builder in the literal sense—he built a large part of the British Empire in Africa. He coined the phrase "Cape to Cairo," became a multimillionaire, and in 1880 founded the De Beers Diamond Company.

Another such man was Barnett Barnato, also from England, but from the London ghetto where his father was a Jewish shopkeeper named Isaacs. Barney Barnato, as he called himself, left the ghetto, came to Kimberley in 1873, and with his brother started a firm of diamond brokers, Barnato Brothers. In 1880 he founded the Barnato Diamond Mining Company, the great rival of Rhodes' De Beers Diamond Company.

An eight-year struggle for control of South African diamonds followed. Rhodes and Barnato each strove to increase the production of his own mines and to capture world markets from the other. Each added to his holdings by

Barney Barnato (above) and Cecil Rhodes (opposite) radiate power and influence.

snapping up shares in lesser diamond companies that could not compete with him. The struggle between the two giants went on until Rhodes persuaded Europe's foremost banking house, the Rothschilds, to throw their financial support to him. The combination of Rhodes and the Rothschilds was unbeatable in South Africa, and in 1888 Barnato admitted defeat. He was still powerful enough to make a lucrative deal in which he transferred his diamond assets to De Beers Consolidated Mining, which Rhodes formed, in return for a permanent seat on the company's board.

Rhodes now had a hammerlock on the South African diamond industry. And he was rapidly dominating the South African gold industry.

That industry skyrocketed in 1886 after a handyman named George Walker discovered gold at Langlaagte, a farm belonging to the Oosthuizen family. Walking through the fields at Langlaagte, Walker tripped over a rock in the grass, looked at it, and saw the telltale signs of auriferous rock.

The Oosthuizen farm lay on the Witwatersrand, the Transvaal's "Ridge of White Waters," so called from the flash floods of the rainy season that sent streams hurtling down the slopes of the ridge. More gold was found, and the Rand (the familiar diminutive of the place) proved to be no false alarm; a reef, or plane of ore-bearing rock, was traced down into the earth.

That was enough to start a gold rush, one that immediately got caught up in the political, social, cultural, and religious complexities of a three-way tug between British imperialism, Boer independence, and the status of black Africans. The human factors that bedevil South Africa in the late twentieth century existed in the early nineteenth century too. We have come to know those factors under the general term *apartheid*, meaning a system of strict racial segregation in which a white minority dominates and rules over a black majority. Apartheid had a long history behind it by the time of South Africa's gold rush.

Dutch settlers founded Cape Town in 1652. The British captured the city in 1795, returned it in 1802, recaptured it in 1806, and in 1814 received its formal cessation by the Netherlands. The Bantu-speaking inhabitants were in the way, and that was the reason for the series of Kaffir Wars (from the Arabic name for infidel given to the blacks) that followed one another until the middle of the nineteenth century when the blacks were decisively defeated.

As the blacks retreated from the British, so did the Boers, who in 1835–36 made their legendary Great Trek north across the Cape Colony to Natal and across the Vaal River to the Transvaal, where they conquered the Zulu tribes that had been fighting among themselves. The British annexed Natal in 1843. The Boers established an independent state

This picture of a market reflects the pastoral atmosphere of pre-boom Johannesburg.

in the Transvaal to which they gave the name South African Republic. The British annexed the Transvaal in 1877, but a rebellion restored the independence of the Boers in 1881. Two years later the masterful Paul Kruger became president of the South African Republic, a position he held when the gold rush began (in 1886) and for the rest of the century.

Kruger saw the rush as an invasion of unwelcome foreigners, most of them British, who threatened the Boer way of life in the Transvaal—a way compounded of a narrow Calvinist creed, belief in white supremacy, hard work, thrift, paternalism, and xenophobia. He particularly disliked the British because their power confronted the Boers across the Vaal River, because they had a record of taking territory away from his people, and because their institutions smacked too much of democracy. Unable to stop the influx, he discriminated against the "outlanders" by levying special taxes on them and by refusing to let them become citizens, discrimination that convinced Rhodes that decency and justice demanded permanent British annexation of the Transvaal.

The first gold seekers to reach the Transvaal were not worried about their political status. The usual motley, international horde of every gold rush, they had come to make their fortunes by digging into the Rand. Nevertheless, they had to obey the law. This was not open, unclaimed land, but rather the preserve of settlers or the government, and leases and licenses had to be purchased before anyone had a right to dig anywhere. The legal documents could not be avoided since the mining commissioner representing the government was on the scene and very much in charge. No Transvaal settler could be ruined as Sutter had been at New Helvetia in California.

Kruger announced in September that public diggings were being thrown open and that those with licenses would be allowed to work claims of about 100 acres each. The fee for a five-year lease was ten shillings a month. The fee caused no trouble between the government and the miners, but the short term of the lease provoked protests from those who thought they might just be realizing their greatest wealth in five years.

Maintaining a tight grip on the mining area, Kruger and his colleagues even decided which mining camp would be the town and, if the gold lasted, the city of the goldfields. They chose a site on a slope of the Rand, so strategically placed that as the mining industry became a permanent boom, the town became not only a city but a metropolis— Johannesburg.

State surveyor Joseph De Villiers, aided by a team of town planners, laid out Johannesburg according to a geometrical design. He made provision for a main thoroughfare seventy-five feet wide, running the length of the town, flanked by 600 plots of land. Side streets branched off at right angles. Some mining claims were inside the limits of Johannesburg, which forced Villiers to mar his geometry to get around them. Later speculation had it that most of the site held gold that should have been sought at the time, gold that now lies irretrievable beneath the massive buildings of Johannesburg.

The planners laid out quarters for the commissioner and his family, a building that included rooms for the post office

Paul Kruger's face mirrors the determination that troubled the British.

and the telegraph. They anticipated the construction of a courthouse, hospital, bank, pharmacy, stores, restaurants, coffeehouses, and schools. They had the foresight to add to their plans a building that in time saw a good deal of use: "A small jail with three rooms. . . . The walls are two feet thick and some ten or eleven feet tall."

The Rand, so recently empty, became the focus of roads across the Transvaal, over the Vaal River into the Orange Free State, and on to the Cape Colony. Newcomers came in by oxcart and carriage until the building of the railroads, which went forward rapidly through the exploitation of nearby coal beds to fuel the locomotives.

On December 8, 1886, the authorities auctioned off the first gold claims. The bids and acceptances were ridiculously low by later standards, the highest being the equivalent of just over $700 for a combination of four claims. Their owners hurried to the goldfields to begin work.

While planning and building went on in Johannesburg, the miners made the site a wide-open mining camp of tents and mud huts. They indulged themselves with cards, hard liquor, and compliant ladies of the evening according to the time-honored rites of such places. Claim-jumping and theft occurred, as did murder and mayhem. The jail became fully inhabited shortly after it went into operation, except when one of the periodic jailbreaks emptied it.

Respectability was represented by a theater where sentimental melodramas like the popular *East Lynne* brought tears to the eyes of hard-bitten miners. Occasionally a circus came to town. The churches arrived, including Dutch Reformed, Presbyterian, Baptist, and Catholic. The Jewish community was so large that its rabbi petitioned for a bigger piece of land than that allotted to the synagogue. The Salvation Army paraded so frequently to the sound of drums and cymbals that the commissioner protested that the band interrupted his work.

Just a year after its foundation, Johannesburg had a population of 6,000. Edward Bok, a South African official, described it as a town of "elegant" houses, of government edifices that would be "imposing" when finished, and "alive" with auctions, brokers, and businesses. Bok had dinner at the Cafe Francais, an indication of the high level to which the taste of some of the residents had risen.

He noted one problem that would continue to vex South Africa, that of the blacks who worked for the miners. They took jobs as laborers at mines where they could not be bosses (a term from the Dutch). Typically for his period, Bok saw the problem as one of unreliable native workers who, corrupted by too much money, would vanish the day after payday to go home or have a spree. His proposed remedy was to pay them by the month instead of the week.

These two pictures (opposite) show Johannesburg in transition from a mining settlement to a commercial urban center.

*Two well-dressed and probably well-heeled men
act out panning for gold in the Transvaal.*

What of the gold miners themselves? All gold rushes of
any size have a common history, in that the early stages
belong to prospectors on a get-rich-quick binge and the later
stages belong to the mining companies. The prospectors pan
and dig the surface gold, and when that is gone, what
remains is beyond their reach. They then give way to the
corporations with the machinery to dig deep down and
wrench out the lower layers of gold-bearing ore.

The Rand shared this history, but it was a special case
because of the enormous ratio of depth gold to surface gold.
The reefs, dropping underground immediately, required
deep mining almost from the start, which meant that capital
had to be raised, machinery purchased, and transportation
developed across 1,000 miles from the Cape to the Transvaal. Individuals and petty groups could not stand the
financial strain. They sold out and vanished from the scene
like minnows fleeing at the appearance of sharks.

The South African gold rush was a millionaire's gold rush.
The participants were not out to strike it rich. They had
already done that. They wanted to increase their fortunes
and, more important, they wanted power. They were captains of industry striving to control one more source of
wealth, to monopolize markets, to dictate terms to rivals,
and to be treated deferentially when they visited world
capitals and financial centers.

Word of Rand gold sounded loud and clear in Kimberley,
where the leaders of the diamond industry turned their
attention to gold. The precious stones they were placing on

the fingers of ladies around the globe gave them the financial
strength to go into the gold industry in a big way, and they
were among the first into the Transvaal.

They were the Randlords.

Barney Barnato came with the intention of buying enough
of the gold areas to make Barnato Brothers dominant (this
being before his alliance with Rhodes). He also acquired
land in Johannesburg on an enormous scale, and what he
had in mind was no less than to establish and control the
business center of the town, complete with a stock exchange
where gold shares would be bought and sold. He accomplished much of this by spending millions. The Barnato
buildings became a center of Johannesburg's financial life.

Not *the* center. Barnato had too many rivals for that.
Alfred Beit, who came from Hamburg and became a tycoon
in Kimberley diamonds, backed the Robinson syndicate
that grabbed a large share of the Rand reefs and the financial
power in Johannesburg. Edouard Lippert's influence came
from his representing a number of companies and their
combined capital. The Ecksteins were there, and Julius
Jeppe, and Sig Neumann. From abroad, the Rothschilds
and the Barings bought shares in the companies that seemed
to them stable at the moment and bound to expand in the
future. The Rothschilds put some of their money into a
company called the Gold Fields of South Africa, organized
in 1887 by Cecil Rhodes.

Rhodes had already laid the basis for his financial
supremacy in South Africa. He wrote to his partner, Charles

By 1888, gold mining in South Africa was no longer the province of the individual prospector.

Rudd, on December 12, 1886: "I shall be glad to hear when you are returning, as between gold and diamonds there is too much to attend to, and I feel I ought not to be leaving De Beers but I am required in the Transvaal." Rudd returned in good time, and the pair juggled their gold and diamonds with much skill.

One problem on the Rand was the slant of the reefs, the auriferous rock, which cut into the earth at an angle. It was hard to tell when a reef gave out and when it had simply dipped away from the mine shaft. The "lost reef" that caused so much speculation as late as the 1930s was found eventually by a new technique, the use of a magnetometer that detected the magnetic shale beneath the auriferous rock. Before then, it was a matter of digging directly down from points on the surface to where one thought the reef cut across—an arduous undertaking, often a failure.

Where the angle of the reef was known and a shaft could be sunk to it, the method of getting at the gold still was difficult. Underground crosscut tunnels were dug from the shaft to meet the reef. More tunnels, called "drives," branched out along the plane of the reef—"raises" angling upward, "winzes" downward. The ore was dug along the raises and winzes. Pried loose, the fragments of rock were taken to the surface for processing.

This method has been in use ever since; and now, as then, it is not a method for any except the big operators, the already rich.

A second problem on the Rand was the nature of the ore. The top layer of a reef usually was made of conglomerate, pebbles held together by a matrix into a ball of hard rock looking something like a cake stuck with currants and containing a minute amount of gold. The Boers called it "banket" because it resembled a kind of gray toffee stuck with white almonds of which they were fond.

The amalgamation method of extracting the gold was to crush the ore, mix it with mercury, which formed an amalgam with the gold content, vaporize the mercury by heating the amalgam in a furnace, and scoop up the gold that remained. Immense masses of conglomerate had to be crushed and amalgamated to produce a tiny amount of gold, another good reason why the Rand has always been a field for syndicates and cartels with heavy machinery, not for the lone prospector with pan and pickax.

But this was only part of the difficulty. Below the conglomerate lay beds of pyritic ore, containing gold, no doubt, but gold coated by iron pyrites that prevented the amalgamation process from working. The gold slipped away in the discarded "tailings" at a ratio too high to make gold mining financially feasible. When this scientific truth registered in Johannesburg, the Randlords went into a crisis of confidence. People left the city in the belief that the golden extravaganza was over. Rhodes himself, shaken by the high percentage of useless ore to salvageable gold, made gloomy predictions about the future of the Rand.

While the Randlords worried, help was on the way from far-off Scotland, where in Glasgow a chemist named John MacArthur and two doctors, William and Robert Forrest, had taken up the challenge of the pyrite. After some experimenting, they developed the MacArthur-Forrest cyanide process that made retrieving gold from pyrite economically sound.

The process, still in use, is based on cyanide's affinity for gold, with which it unites, leaving the rest of the ore aside. The cyanide-gold solution is combined with zinc dust, which replaces the gold in the solution, and the gold is deposited as a black powder. The black powder is mixed

In this Punch *cartoon, Cecil Rhodes is shown astride and in control of Africa.*

with lead, carbon, and carbonate of soda. When this compound is heated, the residue is pure gold.

The MacArthur-Forrest cyanide process reached the Transvaal in time to end the panic among the Randlords, who went into high gear again. The South African gold industry moved into a new era, one that, in spite of downtrends along the way caused by wars, depressions, and crises on the international money markets, has continued through the twentieth century. The gold of South Africa has never given out. On the contrary, the discovery of new reefs has galvanized it several times.

MacArthur and his method arrived in the Transvaal in 1890, the year when Rhodes, who had been elected to the Cape Colony legislature in 1881, became prime minister of the region, a post from which he pressed successfully for northward penetration of British imperialism into black Africa. (Rhodesia took its name from his.)

In 1895, Rhodes played a conspiratorial role in the notorious Jameson Raid, the swoop into the Transvaal by Leander Jameson and his troop of horsemen. Rhodes and Jameson both assumed that the outlanders of the Rand, being mainly British and discriminated against by the Kruger government, would rebel against the Boers and join the British invaders. Perhaps the Transvaal could be taken over then and there; perhaps the hand of the British government would be forced if prolonged fighting took place; in any case, the consummation would be incorporation of the territory into the British Empire.

The plot broke down because no insurrection occurred in Johannesburg. Jameson and his men rode toward the city only to be trapped, defeated, rounded up, paraded through the streets of Pretoria, and jailed—to Kruger's delight, to Rhodes' discomfiture.

While the Jameson Raid was being heatedly debated throughout South Africa, Mark Twain arrived in the Transvaal. The man from Missouri tried to get some one to show him how the raid could have succeeded. At the end he confessed to being baffled, although he did express sympathy for the raiders, evidently because he preferred British ways to those of the flinty, predestinarian Boers.

Recalling his days in the Comstock Lode thirty years before, Twain commented: "I had been a gold miner myself, and knew substantially everything these people knew about it, except how to make money."

On the difficulty of extracting the gold of the Rand: "The successful mines pay great dividends, yet the rock is not rich, from a California point of view. Rock which yields ten or twelve dollars a ton is considered plenty rich enough."

On Johannesburg: "In seven or eight years they have built up, in a desert, a city of 100,000 inhabitants, counting white and black together, and not the ordinary city of wooden shanties, but a city made of lasting material."

Mark Twain continued blithely on his international lecture tour, but Cecil Rhodes had to stay in South Africa and face the music. Condemned in London for complicity in an attack on a friendly nation, he resigned the office of prime minister of the Cape Colony in 1896. He spent much of his time supervising the development of Rhodesia before being reelected to the Cape Colony legislature in 1898. When the Boer War came in the following year, he commanded troops at Kimberley and resisted a long siege by the enemy until a British column broke through and relieved the city on February 15, 1900. Two years later Rhodes died, bequeathing a fortune of £6 million, part of which he had earmarked for the Rhodes Scholarships that continue to bring foreigners to Oxford to study.

A somber Rhodes rests during the Matabele Rebellion (1896), suppressed by his troops in Rhodesia.

A new generation of statesmen was already taking over, of whom the foremost would be Jan Christiaan Smuts, a Boer who raided British lines as a commando, yet who had enough feeling for reality to accept the Transvaal's entry into the British Empire. He twice became prime minister of the Union of South Africa, graduated into being the elder statesman of the empire, and died before he could see his work undone in 1961 when South Africa left the British Commonwealth.

The Boer War caused a hiatus in South African gold mining. Production ceased except for a relatively minor amount controlled by the Transvaal government, which took over the mines and kept a few open. Facing defeat, Kruger fled to Europe in search of aid for the Boers that never materialized. There he died in 1904, leaving unanswered the question: Whatever became of the gold that had been mined during the years 1899–1902? The cost of the war accounted for only part of it. The fate of the rest belongs to the legend of "Kruger's missing millions," to which we will return later (see Chapter 7).

The gold industry revived when the British established their authority over the Transvaal. World War I saw a transformation of ownership of the mines because, after anti-German riots rocked Johannesburg, the government expropriated and sold German properties and assets. In 1919, Ernest Oppenheimer formed the Anglo-American Corporation of South Africa with Wall Street backing and with Thomas Lamont, representing the House of Morgan, on the board. Anglo-American became the new titan of the industry.

Gold reefs continued to be discovered—West Witwatersrand in 1932, Orange Free State in 1939, Evander in 1950. Meanwhile, World War II pointed to an enormously valuable metal never before recognized as such. The atomic bomb popularized the word *uranium*, and the continuing demand for the fuel used in nuclear fission caused a postwar hunt for uranium. South Africa, source of the biggest supplies, experienced a uranium rush—another rich man's rush, dominated by tycoons of diamonds and gold.

Do any more gold reefs remain to be discovered? It seems likely enough that they do, but far underground where they

In Africa, General Jan Smuts (opposite) put down a Boer uprising in 1914 and then battled the Germans. Later as South African prime minister and field marshall (inset), he played important roles in World War II and in organizing the United Nations.

Boer War soldiers man the barricades while the wounded are cared for in the trenches.

are difficult to identify from the surface. In 1946 a shaft sunk in the Orange Free State hit a reef nearly a mile down, one of the richest ever found. Sir Ernest Oppenheimer (he had been knighted in 1921) exulted that another phase in the glittering history of South African gold mining was about to open. Time and deep mining made a prophet of him.

The chief reason for believing that more reefs exist is the pattern of those already known. The Rand complex forms a single gigantic geological system in which there are, in a broken arc extending for hundreds of miles, seven goldfields—Evander, East Rand, Central Rand, West Rand, West Witwatersrand, Klerksdorp, and Orange Free State. That hidden reefs lie in, between, and beyond these fields is a possibility no one can deny.

How deep will the mines go? It seems that they will go where the gold is and as deep as technology will allow.

Today some descend beneath the Rand for two miles, a depth at which the heat alone is a problem, rising from 90° F. at one mile to 130° F. at two miles. Cool air is drawn from the surface, but there is no method of reducing the humidity to a comfortable level since water seeps in from the rocks continually and more water has to be sprayed in the mines to keep the dust down.

In these circumstances, depth miners are carefully selected and trained for the job. Most of the workers, Bantus from the surrounding black territories, volunteer for these mines because they need the pay. Only those get jobs who can pass physical tests under simulated heat and humidity conditions, who have the stamina to labor long hours with heavy equipment for boring and blasting, and who are level-headed enough not to develop pathological fears far underground where work is done between rocky shelves too close together for a man to stand up.

They labor stripped to the waist, beaded with sweat, wearing rough boots and pants, their legs protected by heavy rubber guards, finding their way into the rocky wall by means of the miner's lamps on their hard hats. Straining every muscle, they cut the ore into chunks with pneumatic drills so that it can be raised to the surface and processed for the gold it bears. More than 300,000 of these men work at the rock face or in subsidiary jobs like installing wooden props to help support the ceilings or filling cars with ore for transportation to the bottom of the mine shafts for the long rise to the surface.

Forty thousand white men hold the higher jobs. It takes so many, black and white, because so much ore has to be mined to produce gold in sufficient quantities. The result is certainly worth the effort, for the Rand has given up $25 billion worth of gold since 1886 when the gold rush began.

British cavalry (opposite) stack their guns and care for their mounts during a pause in the Boer War.

Chapter Five

Over the Chilkoot Pass

Klondike-bound prospectors (opposite), heavily laden, plod single file up the thirty-degree incline toward the Chilkoot Pass and into Canadian territory.

If gold rushes are judged by the number of important writers they attracted, then the stampede north along the Trail of Ninety-eight is the greatest of them all. The Klondike had Jack London and Robert Service, and even the diminutive talent of Joaquin Miller added something to the saga; Alaska had Rex Beach; and Hamlin Garland made a resolute effort to reach the goldfields before the hardships caused him to turn back. All five of these men hold a place in literature, and from their writings about the northern wilderness an anthology of ninety-eight can easily be assembled. Hollywood films have been made from their novels, from London's *Call of the Wild* and Beach's *The Spoilers*, to mention two of the most successful productions.

None of these writers, incidentally, made a fortune prospecting in the goldfields of the north. They were less interested in gold than in the adventure itself, and their bonanza came from publishing houses in the United States where editors accepted their manuscripts, paid for them, and saw them through into print. All five have been printed and reprinted, a practical proof of their vitality and durability.

None, however, took for a subject the mystery in which the gold rush of ninety-eight begins. None asked: "Who found the gold that started the stampede north?" This is, nonetheless, a question that the historian cannot avoid, a question that must be asked even though no single answer can be given. Three men at the time claimed for themselves the role of discoverer as did John Marshall in California, William Hargraves in Australia, and George Walker in South Africa, and two of the claimants remain possibilities for the distinction of causing the Klondike fever.

The knowledge that gold existed in western Canada and

Geo. W. Carmack
Discoverer of the
Klondike.

Alaska long antedated this period. The local Indians noticed the yellow metal in the streams and let it lie there since they had no use for it. White men picked up bits here and there, just enough to start small gold rushes in the forty years before the events that caused the convulsion of ninety-eight. The scent of gold drew miners into British Columbia after gold was panned in the Fraser River in 1858. This area remained the focus until 1886 when attention shifted to the Fortymile River, which empties into the Yukon River near Alaska's border with the Yukon Territory. By 1896 hundreds of miners were tramping along the main stream and its feeders, hoping to find much gold where a little had already been found.

They were a small army for a large campaign. The Yukon River, the "Great River" of the Indians who lived along its banks, the fifth largest on the continent of North America, is 2,000 miles long and drains an area of over 300,000 square miles. The river flows northwest from the series of lakes that form its headwaters near the border of British Columbia, and crosses the Arctic Circle, before bending southwest in a sharp angle and following a course through central Alaska until it reaches the Bering Sea. The rivers that join the

George W. Carmack proudly poses (opposite), claiming that he discovered the gold that initiated the Klondike rush.

An 1898 map of the Klondike goldfields was "compiled from the best information available."

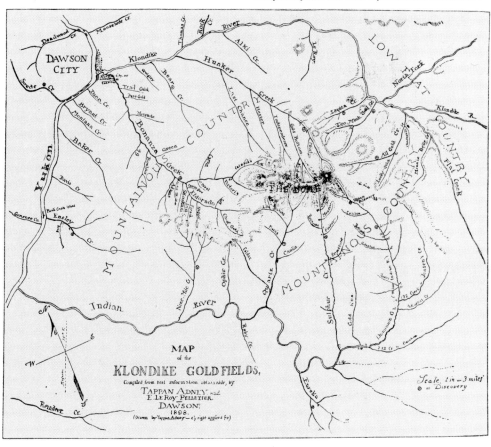

Tons of food and equipment waiting to be claimed clutter the shoreline of Dyea (opposite). Each miner had to have supplies sufficient to last one year when he entered Canadian territory.

Klondikers debark with their supplies from a steamer in the harbor of Dyea, Alaska, onto a scow that takes them ashore.

Yukon as tributaries include the Teslin, Pelly, Stewart, Indian, Porcupine, Tanana—and the Klondike.

The latter name is from an Indian term that sounds something like "Trondiuck" and means "Hammer Water," signifying the method used by the indigenous people to fish for salmon: They hammered wooden stakes into the river bed, strung nets, and gathered the fish that got caught trying to swim upstream to their spawning grounds or downstream toward the open sea. The Klondike gave its name to the gold rush because along its creeks the prologue and the main action of the melodrama were enacted.

The dispute about priority in the discovery of Klondike gold came about in this manner.

Robert Henderson, a sailor from Nova Scotia, was one of the prospectors who during the 1890s had been exploring the Yukon River and its feeder streams in the belief that large accumulations of gold must lie near the areas of earlier modest discoveries. In the summer of 1896 Henderson was on the Klondike, where from one creek he panned enough nuggets to justify a search for more. He named the stream Gold Bottom Creek and departed to make his discovery known to other prospectors, as the unwritten code of the gold seekers prescribed.

This was the basis of Henderson's claim that he discovered Klondike gold.

At the confluence of the Yukon and the Klondike he met George Washington Carmac, an American married to an Indian wife. Carmac was an adopted member of the Tagish tribe, a fisherman and timber cutter, and a part-time prospector for gold. He was salmon fishing with two Indian companions, Tagish Charlie and Skookum ("Strong") Jim, when Henderson came along. Henderson told Carmac about his find at Gold Bottom Creek and encouraged him to stake a claim there, adding at the same time, in an insulting manner, that the Indians were to be excluded.

When Henderson left, Carmac placated his angry Indian companions by saying that together they would look for their own creek. They panned a little gold on the waters of Rabbit Creek before reaching Henderson's camp, where Carmac assured Henderson that he would let him know if anything more interesting than Gold Bottom Creek should come to light. Henderson, still friendly to Carmac, again insulted the Indians by refusing to let them have any of his tobacco.

After failing to find anything significant at Gold Bottom Creek, the Carmac party moved back onto Rabbit (later Bonanza) Creek, looked for gold, ran out of provisions, and sent Skookum Jim to hunt for food. Jim killed a moose on August 16, 1896, went to the stream to drink, and found the sand riddled with gold nuggets, some of appreciable size. It

was a much richer strike than the one Henderson had made at Gold Bottom Creek.

This was the basis of Skookum Jim's claim that he discovered Klondike gold.

It all depends on your definition. If by discoverer you mean the one who stirred the first local interest in the Klondike in 1896, then the distinction belongs to Henderson. If you mean the one who started the wild rush to the Klondike, then the distinction belongs to Skookum Jim.

Carmac, as the white man of Jim's party, staked a claim on Bonanza Creek on August 17. He staked as the discoverer, which gave him title to a double claim, and he insisted afterward that he was the true discoverer of Klondike gold; but Yukon Commissioner William Ogilvie spoke to all of the principals, and he was convinced that the honor belonged to Skookum Jim, who, backed by Tagish Charlie, testified that Carmac persuaded them that Indians would not be allowed to stake claims for themselves.

At any rate, Carmac also staked claims for the two Indians. He did *not* send word to Henderson about the discovery as he had promised, evidently because, as an Indian by adoption and friend and relative by marriage of Jim and Charlie, he resented Henderson's racial slurs. Henderson never forgave Carmac for not letting him in on the Bonanza Creek bonanza.

Floating down the Yukon to Fortymile, Carmac exhibited a cartridge shell of nuggets, described the creek they came from, and declared that plenty more were lying there ready to be scooped up. Within hours Fortymile had lost most of its citizens, who were racing pell-mell for the Klondike River.

The last of the great gold rushes had begun. The familiar story followed. As word spread through the region and then abroad, gold seekers converged from all points of the compass, from each of the continents, from most of the nations of Europe and America, from nearly every vocation, trade, business, and profession.

They came to the Klondike by many trails. From the east, trails out of Edmonton in Alberta took different routes, one a curve by way of Lake Athabasca and Great Slave Lake, and were so long and hard that they soon lost their appeal. The map seemed to indicate that the easiest way would be from the south along the Ashcroft Trail, an all-land route up from British Columbia skirting east of the Coast Mountains, which thus would not have to be crossed. The map lied. On the ground, the Ashcroft Trail was the toughest, 1,000 miles of dark scrub forests, steep hills, quagmires, flies, mosquitoes, little food, and only intermittent pasturage for pack animals. Most of those who took this route dropped out before the end. Hamlin Garland was one of them. He found the Ashcroft Trail worse than the Middle Border of his somber reminiscences.

An all-water route approached the Klondike from the north, by way of St. Michael near the mouth of the Yukon River and then up the river. This was an easy route for the lucky few who could find and pay for places on small boats during the warm months when the river was ice-free and open to traffic. Combined water and land routes allowed travelers to sail north from San Francisco or Seattle through the Inland Passage, to go ashore at different places along the Alaska coast, and to head east for the Yukon on the opposite side of the mountains. Of these, the trails most favored went through the White Pass or the Chilkoot Pass. The landing place for both passes was Skagway, at the head of the Lynn Canal, where the Alaska Panhandle thrusts northward toward the British Columbia-Yukon Territory border.

Skagway in 1896 was a hamlet clinging to the southern shore of Dyea Inlet, a remote place where a few hardy souls

Before rails were laid from the Skagway waterfront to the White Pass, freight was hauled by dogs and men.

lived with salt spray, seaweed, mud flats, sluggish creeks, and a rampart of cold gray mountains frowning down on them from the western horizon. Two years later Skagway had saloons, brothels, gambling dens, piers, warehouses, and a transient population of many thousands, most on their way to the White Pass, twenty miles distant, or to Dyea at the western end of Dyea Inlet, beyond which the Chilkoot Pass offered an entrance to the Yukon.

Skagway, according to American mining engineer T. A. Rickard, was a good place to "take a drink and mush on." Its ways were marked by the usual insensate violence and premeditated crimes of societies made up of adventurers, vagabonds, displaced persons, and get-rich-quick artists, but in addition to that, Skagway had Soapy Smith.

Members of the Soapy Smith gang pose for a group portrait.

Jefferson Randolph Smith came from Georgia. His name suggests respectable, even Southern patrician, origins, and he for a time worked at the respectable trade of a journalist. Respectability, however, was not a trait for which he felt any notable enthusiasm. At the beginning of the 1890s he was in Creede, Colorado, laboring, so to speak, at the more satisfying trade of con man. His gimmick, which gained him his nickname, was to sell a 5¢ bar of soap for 50¢ by advertising that in one of a stated number the fortunate purchaser would find a $5 bill. Somehow the bill always turned up in a bar bought by someone Soapy Smith knew, a confederate who proclaimed his good luck and enticed the gullible into parting with their half-dollars.

Newspaper reports of gold in the Klondike made the con man prick up his ears. Convinced that the reports were true, and as aware as Barnum that a sucker is born every minute, he took passage on a boat to Skagway, where he arrived in the summer of 1897. (He was there when Jack London came through, but London never met or heard of him, so we are deprived of the short story London could have based on this subject.) Within a year Smith levied tribute on Skagway through a gang of sharpers and strong-arm men who specialized in such crimes as robbery, extortion, fraud, shell games, crooked roulette wheels, marked cards, and the rolling of drunks.

Astute enough to restrict most of his operations to "cheechakos," or tenderfeet, who would not hold up their passage through Skagway to the goldfields long enough to testify against him, Soapy Smith still made himself too notorious for the settled population of the town. On July 8, 1898, he and his gang played a con game on a miner just in from the Klondike with a "poke," or bag of gold, which vanished while they were staging a barroom brawl to distract his attention. The victim protested. The gang testified he had lost his gold in legitimate gambling, a story that nobody believed because the veracity of Smith and his men was not something in which anyone had any great faith.

The fraud was too much for the storekeepers, innkeepers, and professional men who feared the archcriminal would ruin them by frightening travelers to the Klondike into bypassing Skagway and landing elsewhere in Alaska. High noon came for Soapy Smith at 8 P.M. on the day of the crime, an hour of full daylight that far north. The citizens called a mass meeting to decide what to do about him. They posted an engineer named Frank Reid to prevent the subject of the meeting from disrupting it, which in fact was his purpose when, carrying a rifle, he marched up to the sentinel. They are said to have exchanged the following words:

Reid: "You can't go down there, Smith!"

Smith: "Damn you, Reid! You have been at the bottom of all my troubles! If I had got rid of you three months ago, I would never have had this trouble!"

Smith attacked Reid, who drew his revolver. A struggle followed in which Smith shot Reid, who managed to fire his revolver before he fell. The bullet killed Smith. Reid, who died shortly afterward, received a hero's funeral and a tombstone bearing the inscription: "He died for the honor of Skagway."

Soapy Smith had been able to "control" the town because he had commanded a band of over fifty desperadoes; nine subsequently went to jail, nine others stood trial but were acquitted, and thirty-five were warned to get out of town. Along with hangers-on, thrill-seekers, and sycophants, Smith had had enough followers to overawe this waystation on the edge of the Arctic where no police force existed. The main issue for the town had not been to enforce the law but to survive the lawless.

By the time of Soapy Smith's passing, Skagway had seen a multitude of cheechakos stop just long enough to pull

Women prospectors also slogged through the mud to seek their fortunes.

Once over the Chilkoot, miners rigged blanket sails on their sleds (opposite, top) and found it easier going across Crater Lake to Dawson. Other prospectors were slowed down by snow storms (opposite, bottom) as they crossed Chilkoot summit.

Overleaf: The long line of pack-laden men struggled up the steep mountainside at the pace of the slowest climber. They slid down. They made four round trips a day for ten days to move the required supplies to the summit on their backs.

themselves together, buy what they needed, and set out for the White Pass, a difficult trail because it led over hills and cliffs, through quagmires, and between gigantic rock formations. Then the crossing of the mountains still lay ahead.

The gold seekers learned it was better to go on from Skagway to Dyea, and to climb the Chilkoot Pass. A relatively clear trail led to the Chilkoot, which, although higher than the White Pass, demanded of travelers one superhuman effort—the conquest of this rift in the mountains itself—and then they were down on the other side in the Yukon Territory.

The Chilkoot Pass was the classical trail of the Trail of Ninety-eight. The scene remains familiar in written accounts and magazine illustrations—a long line of men with heavy packs on their backs struggling in single file up the steep mountainside along the narrow path leading to the pass. Canadian law said each had to bring in sufficient food, clothing, and equipment for one year—over 1,000 pounds of supplies—thus diminishing the possibilty of his becoming a problem for the Canadian authorities. So huge a load had to be broken down into manageable packages, and there was intense competition for Indian porters who were strong enough to carry heavy burdens and who were fast on the trail. Because some Indians had a habit of dropping their loads unceremoniously in order to help somebody who offered a bigger fee, horses were employed wherever possible, but they were few in number and their mortality rate on the trail and over the pass was high.

The packs contained all types of food from vegetables and milk to fresh eggs and live chickens, brought from the south or procured in Skagway or Dyea for exorbitant prices demanded by storekeepers who knew they had the buyers over a barrel. Kegs of liquor were not uncommon. Educated men carried books, writing materials, and musical instruments. Some brought their wives or other women with them. Some women made the trek on their own. Martha Black, who crossed the Chilkoot with her brother, wore the standard feminine attire, blouse, bloomers, and a long corduroy skirt. Bloomers may have been daring in the States but they were mandatory on the trail. Men wore clothing of all kinds from buckskin to the latest San Francisco fashions. One English gentleman brought his valet.

During the season when the Chilkoot Pass was open, the horde of humanity kept coming and climbing. Up and up they went, yard by yard, often on hands and feet, sweating under their packs, cursing the fate that brought them there. The weak, the sick, and the daunted fell out of line, left with nothing but the hope of getting back to civilization. The rest went on through all the hardships, for which they would be repaid, they thought, by the gold of the Klondike. And then

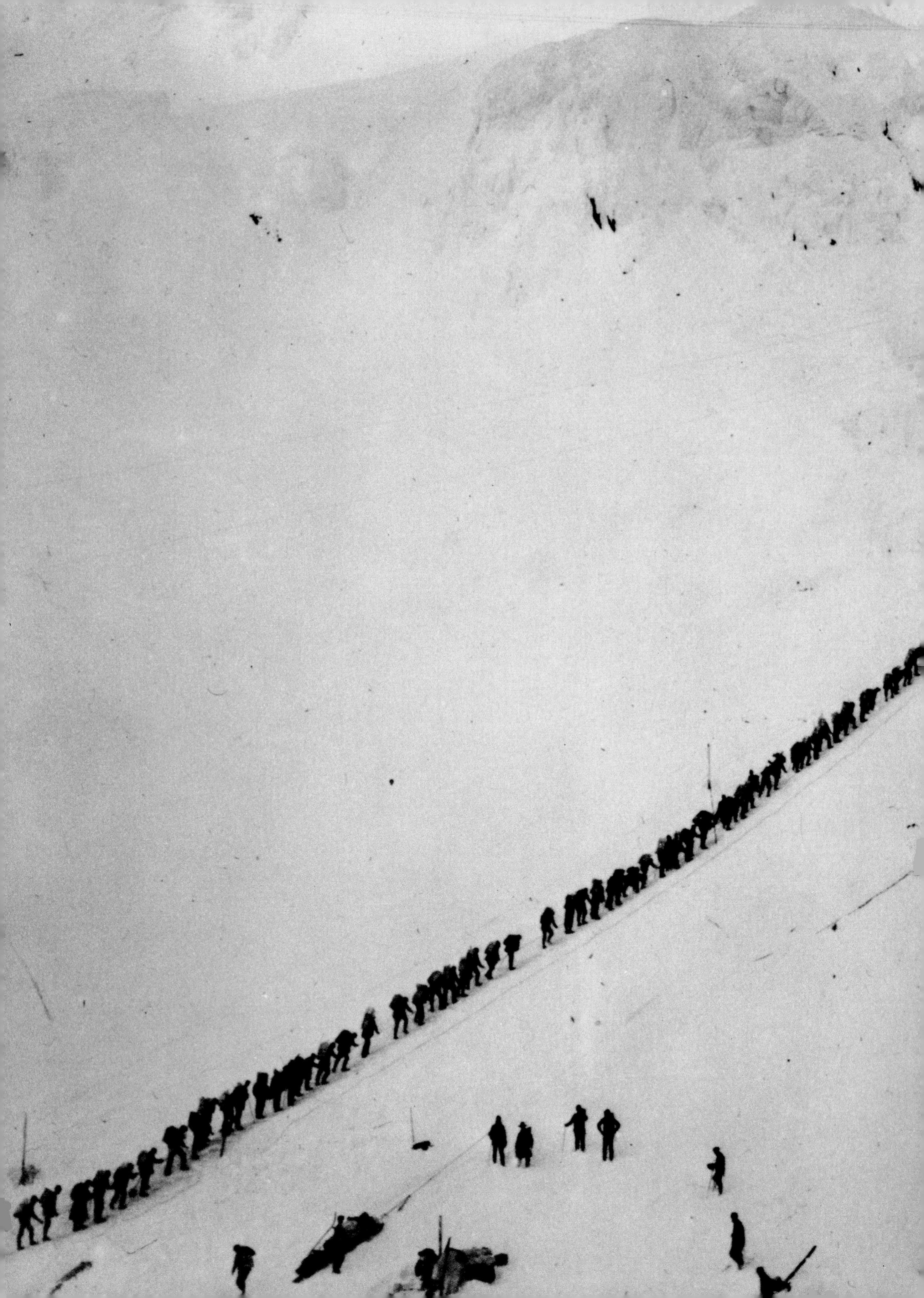

Manpower was the energy source in this case where men hitched themselves to loaded wagons to ford the Dyea River.

came the great moment when they stood on the summit of the Chilkoot Pass and gazed down into the Yukon.

Here the belongings of the travelers were piled high for inspection by the Canadian customs officials, for the mountains divided Alaska from Canada, and foreigners entering the Yukon had to pay duties just like those entering any other part of the country. The Northwest Mounted Police had jurisdiction over the Chilkoot Pass. Impressive in their scarlet tunics, whipcord breeches, broad-brimmed hats, and polished riding boots, they maintained order in the rabble funneling into the pass, examined the baggage as quickly as possible, collected the duties, and waved the newcomers on through.

The descent on the other side of the mountains left the travelers facing another heroic effort if they were to reach the Klondike, 600 miles to the northwest.

Actresses hitched up their skirts to ford the same river. One more enterprising actress also used manpower.

The point about crossing the Chilkoot at all was to reach the upper Yukon. Here small boats could be built from the trees in the surrounding forests for the voyage down the river to the Klondike, but first there was a rocky hike from the Chilkoot to Lake Lindeman, the nearest of the series of lakes where the Yukon River rises. Martha Black wrote of this part of her journey: "The trail led through a scrub pine forest, where we tripped over the bare roots of trees that curled over and around rocks and boulders like great devilfishes. Rocks! Rocks! Rocks! Tearing boots to pieces. Hands bleeding with scratches."

Lake Lindeman connected with Lake Bennett, which could also be reached on foot and was the place where the boating really started. Next came Marsh Lake, out of which the Yukon River takes shape. Below, the dangerous stretch of the river waited, the maelstrom in Box Canyon and

Overleaf: A motley group of Klondike-bound men stand and pose beside their paraphernalia and at the same time watch to see that nothing is stolen.

the raging Whitehorse Rapids. Prudent men, the great majority, went ashore for a portage lasting several days in order to bypass the maelstrom and the rapids. The bolder, who refused to waste that much time and were willing to risk their necks, preferred to try a run through turbulent water lasting a few minutes. Many failed. Boats were swamped or dashed to pieces on the rocks; bones were broken and lives were lost. But still the daredevils pushed off in flimsy craft to defy the Yukon River.

Jack London went through a hair-raising experience, recounted in his "Through the Rapids on the Way to the Klondike," when he and three companions made the run in the *Yukon Belle*, a twenty-seven-footer loaded with their heavy gear as well as with themselves. He wrote:

The Sixty Mile River, really a head reach of the Yukon, flows out of Marsh Lake with a varying width of from an eighth to a quarter of a mile. As it is deep and swift, an idea may be gained of the quantity of water in transit. Suddenly, it narrows to one hundred yards, rounds a bend where a landing may be made in an eddy, and dashes between towering rock walls, about eighty feet apart. This enormous volume of water, thus contracted to so small a passageway, attains a terrific speed, marked by great boilings and upheavals, and waves which stiffly stand up like walls. By some peculiar action or pressure against the rocky sides, the center of the rapids rises up in the form of a backbone, varying from six to eight feet in height. This is called the "ridge."

The trick in running the Box maelstrom was, while hurtling headlong downstream, to stay on the ridge. Although London lashed the steering oar into place, the force of the water carried the *Yukon Belle* off the ridge twice, drenched her crew, threatened to hurl them against one wall of the canyon, and compelled the steersman to use all his strength, skill, and courage to maneuver her back up. They then rode the ridge into calm water and caught their breath.

The Whitehorse Rapids constituted the final obstacle, the hazard being a reef called the "Mane of the Horse" where the only safe channel swung to the right and back to the left creating a thunderous, rampaging whirlpool. London guided the *Yukon Belle* into the channel, where she bounced up and down, careened crazily from side to side, and shipped so much water he feared she would sink. She lurched in a dizzying circle through lashing waves and clouds of flying foam, came back to the open water of the rapids, and dashed through to safety. The rest of the trip down the Yukon was anticlimax.

During 1898 more than 7,000 such boats sailed down the Yukon between May, when the ice on the river broke up, and October, when the weather turned freezing and the ice returned. They stopped at Dawson City, the mining camp and boomtown of the Klondike.

Shooting the rapids (opposite) on the Yukon River between Linderman and Bennet lakes was not exactly a joy ride.

Actresses rest at Happy Camp on the way to the Klondike.

125

At the confluence of the Yukon and the Klondike rivers, Dawson served the mining community that expanded from Henderson's Gold Bottom Creek and Skookum Jim's Bonanza Creek to include the areas of subsequent gold strikes along the tributaries of the Yukon River from the Pelly to the Fortymile. This was par excellence the gold rush of the individual, of the lone prospector who followed a stream until he found "color" in his pan. Partners and small groups worked together too, and they had a chance, for a few years, of becoming rich, before they made way for mining companies and dredges.

The weather and the climate forced the miners to improvise. During the summer months they panned the creeks but could not dig into the sandbars, which lay underwater. During the winter, the sandbars lay exposed but were frozen hard. The solution was to build fires on this rock-hard earth at the end of winter and before the spring floods began. Heat could also be used on the banks of the streams, and from this initial idea two principal methods developed. The first was to shoot flames along the ground from the equivalent of a plumber's torch, a handy method for the individual prospector but too expensive: gasoline, carted from the States, cost too much in the Klondike. The alternative method was to apply steam by means of an iron pipe with holes in the nozzle, attached to a hose that carried the steam from a boiler on the fire. Since wood was the fuel in this case, the steam method was cheaper than the flame method, and it enabled fortunes to be dug up that would otherwise have been inaccessible.

All this shows how different the Klondike was from any other gold rush. Prospectors could adapt smoothly to the circumstances in California, Australia, and South Africa. Not so in the Yukon, a wilderness that had the Arctic Ocean for one of its boundaries. In summer the Yukon was a mush of mud and mosquitos, in winter an icebox in which the temperature would always drop below zero, sometimes to −50°F. The Yukon River flowed through regions never seen by human eyes, the home of the ptarmigan, the polar bear, and the Arctic fox. In the Yukon, special clothing and special housing were needed, and veterans of previous gold rushes were like tenderfeet who had everything to learn. Yukon veterans, the "sourdoughs"—those accustomed to baking bread using fermented "starters" because yeast was unobtainable—had a long head start.

A dance-hall girl (above) and a miner (left) pan for gold on the beach at Nome.

Teams of men (opposite) wash gold-bearing dirt in large riffled sluices. Entire hillsides were dug up, washed, and piled high again.

One miner keeps matters in perspective as he
demonstrates gold panning; the other miners
concentrate on liquor and gambling.

Miners in Dawson (opposite) relax in front of the
Eldorado Restaurant and the Miner's Home.

The cheechakos adapted as best they could. They learned
to wear furs or rough leather, depending on the temperature.
They set up tents in good weather and worked, when they
weren't panning or mining for gold, at felling trees, sawing
planks, and constructing cabins. Winter was coming, the
sub-Arctic winter, when nothing less than a cabin would do.
Here they installed stoves, stored their provisions, squir-
reled their gold nuggets, if any, and added what their
personal needs demanded in the way of bookshelves or other
luxuries of civilization.

On their days off or to celebrate a gold strike, or simply for
the sake of some high jinks, they headed for Dawson, for the
saloons, card games, and dance hall girls of the type
reflected by Robert Service in "The Shooting of Dan
McGrew," the poem that became the tragic ballad of the
Klondike. Service had heard about places like his imaginary
"Malemute saloon" and people like his fictional characters
"Dangerous Dan McGrew" and "the lady that's known as
Lou." He was a bank clerk, born in England and educated at
the University of Glasgow, who arrived by train in Dawson
after the first turmoil of the gold rush, but he captured the
aura of the place and time so perfectly that no one can think
of the Klondike without hearing mentally the jingle of his
facile verses.

129

Women's work is never done, these Dawson women humorously demonstrate.

Entitled "Social Call on One of Dawson's Finest," this picture (opposite, top) shows two party women, Diamond-Tooth Gertie and Cad Wilson, entertaining two friends.

$400,000 of gold dust is escorted by Canadian Mounties (opposite, bottom) on route from diggings to river boats.

Dawson mushroomed overnight into a city with a population of 10,000, three times that number counting all the miners in the goldfields who thought of it as their metropolis. Built low to the water, therefore swampy and subject to flooding, Dawson was often ankle-deep in mud, the reason why its residents laid down boardwalks along the main streets. Major buildings flanked the boardwalks. There were stores, churches, assaying offices, theaters where standard plays were performed, and dives where dance hall girls cavorted in erotic décolletage, bejeweled gowns, billowing petticoats, satin slippers, and titillating garters.

We know much about day-to-day life in Dawson because of *The Klondike Nugget*, which began publication on June 16, 1898. Editor Eugene Allen performed a noteworthy feat just by hauling his press all the way from Seattle to the Yukon, and he overcame the difficulties of publication under conditions that would have made an ordinary newspaperman blanch. Mere delivery of the paper was a continuing difficulty, as Allen noted in an early issue:

Some of the *Nugget* subscribers have been disappointed in not receiving their copies of the paper promptly. To all such we can only offer, as an excuse, the difficulty in locating cabins and places of business which everyone who has attempted to find a particular person has experienced. Addresses as given out in Dawson are often misleading and indefinite. For instance, when the route carrier has to find "the cabin with the screen door," or "the slab house facing the river," or "the big tent with the two stovepipes," or "the cabin three doors south of where all the dogs are," he is very apt to travel some little distance before he finds all the people he is looking for.

The *Nugget* covered local news such as religious and fraternal meetings, food gluts (rare) and shortages (common), and the stringing of the first telephone lines. It gave advice to cheechakos about the necessity of building cabins for the winter and of shifting from rubbers to moccasins in the cold. It counted new arrivals, hailed the building of hotels, restaurants, and theaters, and reported on baseball games and Fourth of July celebrations. It named famous or infamous individuals in town like Joaquin Miller and Calamity Jane. Miller became a contributor to the *Nugget*, for which he wrote "Comrades of the Klondike" with its opening lines about the Chilkoot Pass, "That storm-locked gate to the golden door."

The paper tried to be the gadfly of Dawson, the spokesman of social conscience, as in its protests against the spreading blight of the brothels when girls with trade names like "Spanish Dolores" and "Limejuice Lil" moved their cribs from the Tenderloin to the respectable streets. Allen showed a flair for humor in his coverage of the news. Thus: "Mrs. E. Chronister was a disturber of our quiet little neighboring burg of Klondike City, and Klondike City hooch is not good for staid matrons, as was demonstrated by certain unladylike language. It was a long way to bring her over, so it took $50 and costs to get her back."

There is remarkably little violence reported in the *Nugget* because the Mounted Police were on hand to "get their man" in case of murder, mayhem, or armed robbery. Dawson contrasted with Skagway in this respect. The American town had no law enforcement agency, so that the residents had to fend for themselves against a criminal element of which Soapy Smith was only the worst. The Canadian town had a law against carrying guns; the Mounties enforced it. Smith would have found no field for his talents in Dawson.

The Mounties also patrolled the entire Klondike, not only to control crime but also to bring help to those who needed it, of whom there were many, especially in the winter when the miners were holed up in their isolated cabins waiting for the return of mining weather. Some made good use of this enforced leisure by reading Shakespeare or Gibbon, by writing journals or letters home, or by entertaining themselves on musical instruments. Others killed time by playing cards. All joyfully welcomed men on the trail who stopped for the night.

Some storekeepers, a butcher (opposite, top) and a baker (opposite, bottom), made their fortunes by selling food to miners at very high prices.

Pack horses sometimes were hired to haul goods across the White Pass and the Chilkoot.

The improvident who exhausted their provisions too soon suffered from hunger. Loneliness caused drunkenness, neuroses and hallucinations. Miners cut off for weeks on end by blizzards committed suicide. Partners went stir-crazy and murder resulted. Charlie Chaplin used factual material for *The Gold Rush*, his hilarious, pathetic comedy about ninety-eight: The scene in which he cooks and eats his shoes, the scene in which his hungry cabin mate hallucinates and sees him as a chicken—these could have been realities from the grim annals of the Klondike.

Those who traveled in the wintertime had to endure the rigors of the trail (a phrase Rex Beach used for one of his titles). They went by dogsled, usually with eight or ten animals in the traces, through deep snow and bitter cold. The experienced wore rude goggles over their eyes and patches of rabbit skin on their noses and cheeks. The inexperienced, rash, or unlucky contracted snow blindness or frostbite if they went too far on the trail. The exertion of mushing behind a sled caused profuse sweating; pauses caused chills; and the consequence could be pneumonia. The traveler into the frigid wilderness had to burrow through the snow to find boughs for a fire and a bed, and they were so hard to light that a can of kerosene was a staple of the sled's equipment. The dogs had to be fed, cared for, and kept in their traces because if, 100 miles from nowhere, they fell sick or ran away, their owner might be condemned to a painful and terrifying death.

The Klondike winnowed men as no other gold rush did. All had their failures who gave up, their disappointed who dropped the search for gold and disappeared. None broke or buried as many as the Klondike gold rush. Robert Service, on the hard reality:

This is the Law of the Yukon, that only the Strong shall thrive,
That surely the Weak shall perish, and only the Fit survive.
Dissolute, damned, and dispairful, crippled and palsied and slain,
This is the Will of the Yukon—Lo! how she makes it plain!

Or, as Jack London put it: "A health to the man on the trail this night; may his grub hold out; may his dogs keep their legs; may his matches never misfire." Those who had been on the trail felt a fellowship for those out there at the moment. By the same token, no criminals created more animosity toward themselves than those who committed murder or robbery when they met their victims on the trail.

Another peculiarity that made the Klondike unique was the long night of the winter. The darkness left Dawson in a garish glow of candles and oil lamps, and pedestrians walked past store signs advertising oysters, tobacco, or clothing in a weird setting of lights and shadows. Men and

132

women lost track of time, and the former tended to subside into prolonged debauchery with such of the latter as were willing, whether professionals or amateurs. The red light district never went broke.

Gourmandizing was another feature of Dawson in wintertime. Many people lived from one meal to the next, and complained about food prices that were beyond their means. In the winter of 1898–99, milk sold for $16 a gallon, eggs for $3 a dozen, butter for $3 a pound, and onions for $1.50 apiece; and those were the days when the dollar was worth something, when a good meal could be had for a quarter in San Francisco. Residents of Dawson who lacked the wherewithal for something better subsisted perforce on a diet mainly of sourdough and cornmeal mush.

Wives either adapted to the darkness and the scarcity or abandoned their husbands and went home. Respectable single women had a hard time when they were thrown on their own. One, whose husband had been killed on the Chilkoot Pass, gathered up her courage, went into a saloon alive with loud laughter and dense with tobacco smoke, sang familiar ballads in a trembling voice for miners and hussies congregated therein, and found they liked her so much that she could maintin herself and her young child in comparative comfort on the gold they gave her. Another, who may or may not have been, as her sign proclaimed, "Madame Rousseau from Paris," made a living by laboring long hours every day except Sunday as a "dressmaker and milliner."

With the end of the bad weather, the pans and rockers, long toms and sluices, pickaxes and shovels, went into action again on the banks of the Klondike and its tributaries. The rush to stake claims soon caused the best creeks to be divided up, peacefully, on the whole, because the Mounties kept track of the claims. The Canadians used a number system that simplified the process—One Bonanza, Two Bonanza, and so on.

The richest creek in the long run was the Eldorado, staked first by an Austrian named Antone Stander. So loaded with gold was the ground just a few feet below the surface that prospectors abandoned lesser sites to invade this creek. Thirty Eldorado surrendered $5,000 worth in one day. Alexander MacDonald, who owned this claim and many more, leased his holdings, took a percentage of the gold, and became the "king of the Klondike." The *Nugget* reported these figures on the Klondike for one season: "Eldorado, $2,500,000; Bonanza, $2,500,000; French Hill, $1,600,000; Gold Hill, $1,500,000; Big Skookum, $1,000,000; Little Skookum, $1,000,000; Dominion, $4,000,000; Hunker and Quartz, $5,000,000. Total— $19,000,000."

Lucky miners thought up ways to flaunt their luck.

Dressed in their finest clothes, Dawson citizens pose in front of the Northern Commercial Company.

Clarence Berry put a can of gold and a bottle of whisky outside his cabin and a "Help Yourself" sign next to them. Dick Lowe insisted on treating all present when he entered a saloon, a restaurant, or a brothel. Swiftwater Bill Gates bought up all the eggs in Dawson because his girl friend, Gussie Lomore, had an inordinate taste for them. It was common for a man with a bag of gold to pour his nuggets out on a bar, table, or counter in order to dazzle the onlookers.

What of the four men who started the furor in the Yukon? Carmac took enough gold from his claim to "go outside" to Seattle and high living. Tagish Charlie became rich, the richest man in Carcross, up the Yukon, to which he retired. Skookum Jim, just as rich, never overcame a passion for prospecting, and he lived as hard a life on the trail as he had before his discovery. Only Henderson, who sold his claim for $3,000 (it realized nearly half a million for its new owner), failed to strike it rich, a fact for which he blamed

Carmac for the rest of his life; he complained incessantly that if Carmac had only sent him word from Rabbit Creek, he too would have gone there and made a killing.

There were failures in the Klondike, and successes who threw their money away, and bankrupts who ended up as poor as when they started. Some who cut no figure at all in Dawson found fame and fortune back in the States: Tex Rickard, the sports promoter who presided over the first million-dollar gate when he matched Jack Dempsey and Georges Carpentier in 1921; Sid Grauman, who established his fashionable Grauman's Chinese Theater in Hollywood and recorded the footprints of the stars in wet concrete; Key Pitman, who became senator from Nevada and chairman of the Foreign Relations Committee.

The romance of the rush pretty much ended when the railroad began carrying passengers from Skagway to Dawson over the White Pass in 1900, making unnecessary the harrowing crossing of that pass or the Chilkoot. Four years later the individual miner was in retreat from the companies. The period 1899–1904 is always tabulated for its fantastic production: $100 million of Klondike gold. After that, the figure diminished and men were leaving the Yukon instead of piling into it.

Dawson went from a population of 10,000 in 1899 to 3,000 in 1911 and less than 1,000 in 1921. It took the nostalgia of the mid-twentieth century to bring the town back to something like its old opulence.

By 1900, Dawson had ceased to be the lurid boomtown of its first golden years partly because of two fires that created havoc in 1898 and 1899. The first destroyed about fifty buildings. The second was much worse: the loss in buildings was over 100, the dollar loss over $1 million. This inferno began above the Bodega Saloon in the room of Helen Holden where she entertained her masculine clientele. The fire broke out on a windy night and the flames quickly got out of hand, whipping from one wooden building to another in the center of town. The account in the *Nugget* is so meticulous that much of Dawson could be reconstructed from its account. In one area:

From the Aurora restaurant to the Aurora saloon was short work for the flames, notwithstanding the brave stand made by men on top of the buildings with pails and blankets.

Meantime the long Tivoli building had communicated the heat and roaring flames to the cabins in the alley at the rear, occupied by members of the demi-monde, and leaped from cabin to cabin without let or hindrance. The Aurora Saloon and Hotel made a terribly hot fire which leaped over Second Street, and the two-story building of the Victoria saloon, gambling house and restaurant was involved, as if by magic, causing serious danger to the throngs of men who lined her roof in an effort to prevent the fire from communicating. Up Front Street went the flames, the Northwest Trading Company being the next to go. Then the Madden House, then a grocery store, then the Ryan boot and shoe store, then Graf the jeweler, then the Douglas boot and shoe store; the M and M news stand followed, then the Arlington saloon, followed by the Montana restaurant. Some small buildings in course of erection were torn out and the devastation on the east side of Front Street was stayed at the building of McPherrin and Johnston occupied by the Oregon Store.

Dawson was quickly rebuilt, but it never looked the same again. The new buildings were stronger structures, more regularly laid out, and a number of names changed, newcomers taking over from those who had lost everything, including the heart to continue. More glass was in evidence, more space, more respectability. Oldtimers might deplore the waning of the "anything goes" attitude of the rowdy days, but life for all Dawson was more comfortable, something for which most residents were profoundly grateful.

Many miners, unable to find gold in the Klondike, began to head westward as early as 1899, participating in the rush back across the Coast Mountains to Alaska following the discovery of gold in the Seward Peninsula in 1898. There the interesting commodity was beach gold—gold pounded into the sand by the surf. The waterline being open to all, claims did not have to be formally registered or legally ratified, and as a result the beach was an anthill of men and equipment, a turmoil of movement back and forth into the surf as the tide rose and fell. The difficulties in filtering the sand in the surf brought dredging machines to the beach almost at once. Rex Beach was in the middle of the turmoil:

When that hysterical army was dumped ashore together with mountains of freight, fuel, mine supplies and building materials, the chaos can be imagined. Nome itself, a thin row of saloons, dugouts and canvas shelters, lay like a wagon track between the surf and a treeless, spongy tundra that ran back to a low range of inhospitable hills. Into the wet moss and mud one's boots sank to the knees; aside from the sandy beach there was not a dry place to stand and, of course, nobody had time to sit down.

Nome grew to a boomtown of 20,000. But the gold taken from Alaska amounted to only $2,500,000 in five years, so that this gold rush never rivaled the Klondike, and fewer fortunes were made. Still, there were heroics and dramatics on the shores of Bering Strait and inland, and fortunately Beach was there to record those hectic times in his fiction and nonfiction. Then Nome declined like Dawson back into its native somnolence, waiting for revival in the later twentieth century.

That revival is based on tourism. The Klondike, Dawson

The sands of the beaches at Nome were laced with gold. Two miners work their sand rocker sifting for gold.

in particular, is devoted to preserving the memory of the gold rush by maintaining and restoring old buildings, by reviving the life of the miners in saloons and dance halls (minus the sordid, the tragic, and the unprintable), and by holding dogsled events. Thousands of visitors come in a new gold rush and pour out their money to savor the thrills of the past. They pan for nuggets along the creeks of the Klondike River. They visit derelict cabins where miners waited out the winter. They run, for entertainment, the river that Jack London ran in earnest. They relive and fantasize about the Trail of Ninety-eight through the verse of Robert Service, ending with his salute to those who had been there for real:

> You may recall that sweep of savage splendour,
> That land that measures each man at his worth,
> And feel in memory, half fierce, half tender,
> The brotherhood of men that knew the north.

Chapter Six

Smugglers and Thieves

As gold has been prized since the beginning of the human experience, as it has been sought, cherished, and displayed, just so has it been stolen, smuggled, and used in immoral or illegal ways. The gold thief is always with us.

Not everyone in prehistoric times could find gold, any more than could everyone in later centuries. Even professionals of the great gold rushes came away empty-handed, and we must infer that failure in the hunt has always been a reality that left some human beings disappointed, resentful, and envious. Moreover, there have always been those too lazy or too crafty to search, yet still determined to possess the lustrous, gleaming, fascinating metal. The same means of satisfying this passion for ownership has been tried over and over again: Take the gold you want from somebody who already has it. Steal it!

The first examples of gold robbery of which we have any record are revealed in royal tombs of ancient civilizations. We think of the Egyptians and Sumerians as people dominated by their priestly castes to a point where no individual would dare to violate the taboos or risk the curses laid on them by their religion. Surely the combination of religion and royalty would protect the tombs of their kings?

The truth is that for some individuals the lure of gold outweighed whatever fears they may have felt. Grave robbing began almost as soon as the graves were filled in or the tombs sealed.

Leonard Woolley discovered at Ur in Mesopotamia that the Sumerian workmen who dug the grave of Queen Shub-ad next to that of her late consort, King A-bar-gi, pillaged the earlier grave and took away the gold it contained. The men who committed the desecration must have been an irrever-

ent and cool-headed lot. Risking the penalties if they got caught and ignoring the taboos, the disfavor of the gods, they broke through a brick wall between the graves, swept up all the valuables in the king's sepulcher, among which, judging from Sumerian practice elsewhere, gold objects would have been conspicuous, and made off with their plunder. They probably disposed of it by melting down the gold since the pieces would have been identifiable and therefore too dangerous for them to keep.

The Sumerian experience suggests that the same men who dug the graves, furnished them, and placed the corpses in them also violated them. These men knew where to look and how to get in. The speed of the robberies indicates that they either acted on their knowledge or passed the word to accomplices.

The situation in Egypt is known more fully because of the centuries when elaborate royal tombs were cut into the rock in the Valley of the Kings on the left bank of the Nile near Thebes. Here final resting places of the dead pharaohs held the objects they would need for their final journey, and, as the tomb of Tutankhamen shows, these objects included many of gold. The contents of the tombs were well known to the people of the city as well as to the workmen since the mummy and its attendant artifacts were carried in a solemn procession that crossed the river from Luxor to the Valley of the Kings within the sight of the crowds that lined the route.

Grave robbers went to work shortly after the tomb was sealed in so many cases that the Egyptian authorities became alarmed about the wrath of their deities, who were presumed to be the chastising force behind floods, droughts, and other misfortunes. The civil authorities appointed inspectors to police the tombs, and the priests formulated terrifying maledictions against desecrators. Yet the tombs continued to be visited in the dead of night, stealthily opened, and pillaged.

In modern times the Valley of the Kings revealed so many despoiled burial places that archaeologists questioned whether any had escaped. Howard Carter therefore created a sensation among his colleagues as well as among laymen when he uncovered the tomb of Tutankhamen and found it almost intact. The tomb had been entered, probably soon after the burial, by robbers who removed gold, jewels, and costly oils, leaving empty mountings and vases as witnesses. A tangle of treasures—somewhat tidied, presumably by the necropolis guards who sealed the chambers after the early thefts—remained untouched and unseen from that time until our own.

A documented scandal involving grave robbing rocked the land of the Nile during the reign of Rameses IX (about 1100 B.C.). According to the records, the mayor of Thebes,

In the Valley of the Kings, Carter found the entrance to King Tutankhamen's tomb (opposite). In the tomb, Anubis, god of the dead (top), guarded the innermost chamber. Treasures found in the antechamber (bottom) were in disarray.

having discovered that a number of tombs, both royal and of the nobility, had been violated, informed the vizier of Egypt, the chief adviser of the pharaoh. A dragnet was thrown out and a band of suspects got caught in its meshes. The records seem very modern when they record that the suspects were taken to the scene of the crime, which was reconstructed by having them describe how they had broken into the tombs, what they had taken, and how they had escaped.

The vizier presided over the trial in a temple of the goddess of justice, but when all the facts had been laid out for his inspection, he suddenly called a halt. His motive is another reason for the feeling of modernity one gets in considering this scandal. The testimony of the grave robbers implicated some Theban officials, one of whom was the man responsible for the district in which the tombs lay. There were charges of a cover-up and countercharges of false and defamatory accusations. The evidence was getting too close to implicating the vizier himself when he stopped the trial.

Nearly 2,000 years later there was another grave-robbing scandal in Egypt. In 1881 Gaston Maspero, director of antiquities in Cairo, finding that archaeological digs were being looted, protested to officials of the government. Suspects were brought in, questioned, and then exonerated by the testimony of character witnesses, including Egyptian officials supervising the sites. Naturally some of these officials knew about the stealing of artifacts and had taken their cut of the proceeds. Only a falling-out among the thieves, one of whom confessed, prevented the case from being dismissed. The more things change, the more they remain the same.

While robbing royal tombs was the spectacular type of gold theft in the ancient world, the stealing of gold objects by one person from another remained what it has been ever since, the commonest form of this crime. Rings, bracelets, brooches, earrings, and similar ornaments have been pilfered from their rightful owners in all ages. When gold coins came into use, the clipping of coins, the slicing or chipping off of bits of gold, became a serious crime barbarously punished, for this debased the currency and caused problems for governments. The emperors of Rome, the kings and queens of medieval and modern Europe, all took steps to protect their gold supply because they needed it to meet the expenses of ruling their empires, kingdoms, or fiefs. And rulers did not disdain to steal gold from one another under the guise of state policy.

The thirst for gold led Queen Elizabeth I into her clash with Philip II of Spain. Elizabeth ranked among the Protestant leaders of Europe, Philip among the Catholic leaders, and both required gold for their own forces and to subsidize their allies. Philip had all the gold he could use,

(Opposite, top) The beautiful second coffin is raised from the outer coffin by use of pulleys. (Opposite, bottom) Lord Carnarvon watches Carter wrap one of the wooden statues prior to removing it from the tomb.

(Above) Carter studies the second shrine. (Below) A group of dignitaries watch Carter unwrap the mummy of the king.

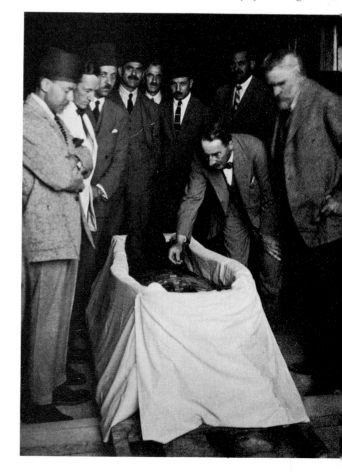

the product of his mines in Mexico, Peru, and Central America. Elizabeth had too little. She decided, in one of the important decisions of her reign, to make Philip contribute gold to her national coffers.

The Spaniards, waging war in the Low Countries, paid their troops by sending gold from Spain by sea. In 1568 one of their treasure fleets carrying an enormous fortune, perhaps the equivalent of about $1 million today, in ducats, the gold coins of the period, took refuge from a storm by running into English seaports. Elizabeth seized the ducats, most of which she dispatched to her Protestant allies on the Continent. A bonus accrued to her in that the Duke of Alba, commanding the Spanish forces in the Netherlands, had to find another source of money to pay his soldiers, and, by imposing a tax on the area, he helped to provoke the rebellion of the Dutch that gained them their independence from Spain.

The desire for gold also lay behind Elizabeth's connivance with Drake, Hawkins, Frobisher, and all the English "sea dogs" who preyed on Spanish commerce. The viceroys of the king in Madrid sent galleons loaded with gold from the New World, great unwieldy cargo ships that were fair game on the high seas. In 1563 English sailors boarded a galleon off Cape St. Vincent and removed its gold. This kind of thing continued in what was an undeclared war.

The career of Sir Francis Drake is the most famous in the history of Elizabethan seafaring. Before the Armada, the Spanish invasion fleet, sailed, Drake scoured the seas for Spanish galleons. During his voyage around the world he captured a ship with so rich a cargo of gold and silver that he used the treasure to ballast his ship, the *Golden Hind*. These depredations contributed to Philip's decision to send his Armada against England in 1588, with the consequences familiar to us all. So much effect did gold have on crucial international events.

The sea dogs were quasipirates hiding behind the shield of royal favor, which gave them a kind of legitimacy in their own eyes if not in those of their victims. True pirates who looted Spanish galleons for themselves appeared in the following century. They roamed the Spanish Main from their bases at Tortuga, Jamaica, and other Caribbean islands, and their preference for galleons came entirely from the knowledge that these were the vessels most likely to be carrying cargoes of gold. Except for that, the pirates were not particular about whom they stopped or raided. Merchantmen of all nations attracted them. They boarded many a craft from which the only gold they took was in the form of gold rings and other jewelry from the passengers.

Friendly Indians offer gold to Columbus.

Galleons (opposite) are provisioned in Lisbon in 1590, before they depart for the New World.

144

*Three of Queen Elizabeth's stalwarts,
Cavendish, Drake, and Hawkins, pose for
posterity.*

*(Opposite, bottom) Sir Francis Drake's fleet
anchors in Cartegena, Colombia. (Opposite, top,
left) The Golden Hind, Drake's flagship,
captures the Spanish treasure ship,* Nuestra
Señora de la Concepción. *(Opposite, top, right)
Anchored off the coasts of Java and Sumatra,
Drake presents his respects to the king.*

Caca Fogo.   Caca Plata.

SVMATRA.

IAVA
MAIOR.

Celebes

Draco.

INSVLA TERNATE.

CARTAGENA

Captain Henry Morgan helps destroy a Spanish fleet guarding Lake Maracaibo.

(Opposite, top, left) Morgan is portrayed as a prosperous gentleman. The Barbarossas (opposite, top, right), operating out of Algiers and Tunis, attacked ships that chanced along. (Opposite, bottom) Morgan's ship blows a French galleon out of the water.

The pirate who looms most formidably across the years was Henry Morgan. A Welshman who served in the British navy, he rose to command his own warship, and turned buccaneer when assigned to the Caribbean. In 1761, sailing from Jamaica, Morgan landed on the Isthmus of Panama at the head of 2,000 men and marched through the jungle to Panama city on the Pacific side. The Spaniards outnumbered the invaders and had cavalry. Morgan did not, but rallied his men, placed his musketeers where they could decimate the enemy, won a furious battle outside the walls, and burst into the city at the head of his men.

His object was Spanish gold, much of which started the voyage to Spain in Panama. Mad with rage when he discovered that most of the gold had been taken away and hidden, Morgan ordered the city to be sacked and put to the torch. By the time he called his men off, it was a mass of glowing embers and seared masonry, and its people were cowering in the jungle. In spite of his failure to find the real hoard of gold, he carried enough of the precious metal away to load a donkey train. Recalled to London to account for this deed, he explained himself so persuasively that Charles II knighted him and sent him back to the Caribbean with the title of lieutenant governor of Jamaica. From then on Sir

S.^r HEN: MORGAN

HORUSCE en HAREADEN BARBAROSSA
Coninghevan Tunis en Algiers en opper Zee vooghde

Henry Morgan displayed a commendable prejudice against pirates, whom he punished whenever they were caught and brought into his jurisdiction.

The city he ravaged never recovered. Returning, the Spaniards found the destruction too great to permit rebuilding on the old foundations. They established another city of the same name on another site. The gold Morgan missed, however, did not return to the new Panama. It remains one of the lost treasures, a cache waiting for a lucky discoverer to find it (see the next chapter).

Later pirates extended their theater of operations. Captain Kidd roamed the Indian Ocean. Blackbeard, whose name was Edward Teach, patrolled the Carolina coast on the lookout for coastal shipping and vessels from abroad. Both of these men were credited with huge hauls of gold, but the rumors have never been verified.

As late as the nineteenth century, a notable pirate operated on the Texas coast, Jean Lafitte, who in 1815 joined his band of corsairs to the American forces of Andrew Jackson at the Battle of New Orleans. Lafitte, who had his lair at Galveston, took gold from Spanish ships and towns of the Gulf of Mexico and the Caribbean.

As late as the twentieth century, pirates were at large in

Two notorious female pirates, Anne Bonney and Mary Read, made history in the Caribbean.

Chinese waters. They infested the river mouths and the coastline and in some cases they, like the warlords in the interior of China, levied a tribute of gold on the cities.

No account of the pirates would be complete without two female marauders, Anne Bonney and Mary Read. Anne absconded from her father's plantation in South Carolina and went to sea aboard the ship of Captain Jack Rackam, a notorious pirate who prowled the Caribbean. Mary Read, a Londoner, was aboard a sailing ship captured by Rackam. She joined him, so that the piratical captain had two women among his crew. A British warship captured the ship in 1720 and escorted it to Jamaica, where Rackam and company were hanged. The two sisters of the Spanish Main received prison sentences and vanished from history.

The pirates of the land in the modern world have been the bandits, the highwaymen, the outlaws. The bandits of Renaissance Rome stopped rich wayfarers on their palfreys and relieved them of bags of gold so often that the time came

*Dick Turpin, the infamous highwayman,
escapes his pursuers.*

when no one carrying anything of value would travel through
the isolated parts of the city without an armed escort. In
England, Dick Turpin made a name for himself as *the*
highwayman by stopping coaches on the King's Highway
and removing from the passengers whatever gold they
carried along with the rest of their valuables. Turpin worked
Hounslow Heath near London, hid out around the heath
when on the run, and secreted his loot where he could safely
return and reclaim it. Some of these caches remained
unclaimed when they hanged him in 1739. One, a basketful
of gold coins, was discovered behind a staircase at the
Bedford Inn.

The outlaws of the American West began with Joaquin
Murieta, the vengeful Chicano of the gold rush of forty-nine
who waylaid Anglo and European miners and took their gold
before his violent death in 1853. Murieta passed the torch,
in a manner of speaking, to Rattlesnake Dick, designer of
the biggest gold hijacking of the era.

Two of the Daltons, Charles (above, left) and Grant (above, right), look fierce and determined.

In 1856, Rattlesnake Dick learned that a shipment was moving down from the northern mines of California by mule train rather than stagecoach because it had to take a steep, narrow trail through rugged mountains. A slow-moving mule train, even one accompanied by guards, was too good a prize for a gold-hungry outlaw to let go by. Dick positioned one group of his gang at a high, lonely spot where they could hide in the underbrush. He took one man with him on a foraging expedition for mules to replace those bearing the transportation company's brand.

The first part of the plan worked without a hitch. The outlaws jumped the mule train, held up the guards, and unloaded the gold for removal to a nearby rendezvous. The second part of the plan failed. Dick and his companion, caught mule stealing, were in jail when they should have been in the mountains. The leader of the hijacking, commanding too few men to carry the entire haul—$80,000 in gold—to a safe place, decided to bury half and take the rest to a hideout near Auburn. A posse ambushed them and recovered the gold in their possession. Since no one talked, the other $40,000 may still lie where they buried it.

In later decades Jesse James, the Younger Brothers, the Dalton Gang, and similar marauders of the Midwest held up trains and banks in a quest for gold. The leading practitioner of gold robbery, however, was a man who operated in the same region as Murieta and Rattlesnake Dick. This was the redoubtable Black Bart, famous in California banditry for his courtly behavior toward women, his poems, and his success in waylaying stagecoaches in the gold country.

Armed with a shotgun and peeping through the eyeholes of a flour sack over his head, Black Bart stopped about thirty stages during the 1870s and 1880s. He specialized in ambushing the Wells, Fargo express. He would order the driver to "throw down the box," which he would retrieve, then retreat to a safe place where he could force the lock and appropriate the contents. In 1877 on the Russian River, and in 1878 near Quincy, he netted consignments of gold coins being delivered by Wells, Fargo. More of the same followed.

This photograph, found in a New Mexican saloon, purportedly is of Jesse and Frank James and their mother.

REWARD!

WELLS, FARGO & CO.'S EXPRESS BOX, CON-
taining $160 in Gold Notes, was robbed this morning, by one man, on the route from Sonora to Milton, near top of the Hill, between the river and Copperopolis.

$250

And one-fourth of any money recovered, will be paid
for arrest and conviction of the robber.

JOHN J. VALENTINE,

San Francisco, July 27, 1875.   General Sup't.

One posted notice offers a $250 reward; another, an invitation to a "neck-tie party."

(Opposite) If history did not tell us otherwise, outlaw Black Bart's elegant, somber dress would make us think he was an honest man.

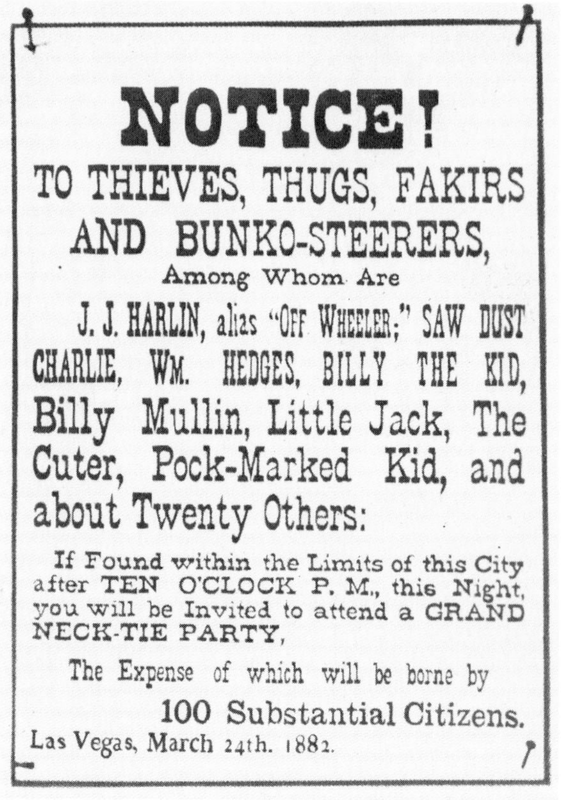

NOTICE!

TO THIEVES, THUGS, FAKIRS AND BUNKO-STEERERS,
Among Whom Are

J. J. HARLIN, alias "OFF WHEELER;" SAW DUST CHARLIE, WM. HEDGES, BILLY THE KID, Billy Mullin, Little Jack, The Cuter, Pock-Marked Kid, and about Twenty Others:

If Found within the Limits of this City after **TEN O'CLOCK P. M.,** this Night, you will be Invited to attend a **GRAND NECK-TIE PARTY,**

The Expense of which will be borne by

100 Substantial Citizens.

Las Vegas, March 24th. 1882.

The company in self-defense began bolting the strongbox to the floor of the stage, which compelled the bandit to hold all on board under the gun while he finished the job on the spot, a hazardous undertaking that he got away with several times but that undid him in the end.

In 1883 he boarded a Wells, Fargo stage and stayed long enough to force the strongbox and take his richest haul, made up of unrefined gold, gold dust, and gold coins. Although he escaped with the booty, during his labors he dropped a handkerchief bearing the mark of a San Francisco laundry. It was elementary for the police to find the laundry, determine the name of the handkerchief's owner (Charles Bolton), and track him down. He did time in jail and, on being released, went into other lines of work.

Black Bart never robbed a lady, and when one in a fright tossed him her handbag from a stage, he gallantly returned it to her unopened. As for his being a poet, he derived much satisfaction from explaining his motives in doggerel. This delicate rhyme from his pen has made the anthologies of light verse:

I've labored long and hard for bread,
For honors and for riches,
But on my toes too long you've trod,
You fine haired sons of bitches.

154

Another kind of outlaw committed the classical gold crime of the nineteenth century. Jay Gould, corrupt financier and railroad wrecker, masterminded a scheme that called for nothing less than making the president of the United States an (unsuspecting) accomplice.

It was in 1869, as Ulysses S. Grant was beginning his first administration, that Gould and his partner, "Jubilee" Jim Fisk, resolved to corner the gold market. They would buy all the gold they could get their hands on, hold it until scarcity caused the price to shoot up, and then dump it on the market. They calculated, correctly, that they could realize an immense profit in a few days.

Success depended on the president holding back the government supplies of gold. Through the president's brother-in-law, Gould got to Grant and persuaded him that withholding gold from circulation would increase the value of gold in Europe and thus raise the prices of American goods abroad, giving the American economy a boost at a time when the farmers especially needed an effective move in Washington to get them out of the doldrums. Accepting Gould's argument, Grant cut off the flow of gold from the Treasury into the marketplace and opened the way for Gould and Fisk to move forward into the second phase of their conspiracy.

The plotters began to buy gold wherever it was to be had, borrowing on their credit to do so. Under their assault the amount of gold in circulation rapidly diminished. The price soared. Wall Street became puzzled, then concerned, then frightened. On Black Friday, September 24, 1869, panic hit the stock market because the price of gold was astronomical and the amount available was too small to suffice for the daily business of the exchange.

Gould and Fisk, delighted that everything was going according to plan, prepared to sell their gold when the market opened after the weekend. They would have made their killing except that the secretary of the Treasury alerted the president to the disaster on Wall Street. Grant, mortified

The gentlemanly poses of Jim Fiske (opposite) and Jay Gould (above) were facades for fiscal chicanery. The cartoon of Fiske (left) depicts him in a truer light.

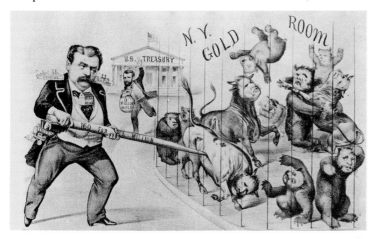

Overleaf: Gold speculators mill about in front of the New York Stock Exchange.

by his own gullibility, released $4 million in gold, bringing the price down sharply. The stock market came back to normal, and Gould and Fisk had the fruits of their plot snatched from them at the last moment.

Some heads of state and government leaders have been the principals rather than the dupes in gold plots. In our time crowned heads have, while still in power, prudently transferred gold from their national treasuries to banks in Europe against the evil day of their fall. Pushed from their thrones, they have gone to Rome or the Riviera, taken command of the gold, and paid for an expensive life-style. King Farouk of Egypt, King Zog of Albania, and Emperor Bao Dai of Vietnam all did this, and spent their last years living like the royalty they once were.

The collapse of Hitler's Reich at the end of World War II produced numerous tales of vast gold stores vanishing in the confusion of defeat, invasion, and occupation. More than 700 bars of gold from the Reichsbank were said to have been loaded on trucks and taken into the Bavarian Alps to be hidden so that the Allies would not get them. These bars have yet to be discovered. Another story states that Nazi gold worth hundreds of millions of dollars was sent into Austria, a second hoard that disappeared without trace. While it is true that quantities of gold, stolen by Nazis bent on salvaging something from the ruin of their cause, have been found in various places in Germany, the immense amounts that have been mentioned appear to be mere fantasies.

Some Nazis who fled to foreign countries did bring gold out with them by resorting to an old method of getting commodities across national borders—smuggling. Most countries have laws governing the movement of gold in and out, and smuggling under normal conditions is difficult if only because of gold's weight; but the conditions in the aftermath of the war were decidedly abnormal, and Germans took advantage of the breakdown to sneak themselves and their gold into South America and elsewhere. That is why so many lived so well without a discernible source of income.

Smuggling today is a way of life in Dubai, on the shore of the Persian Gulf, for the reason that India, across the Arabian Sea, has stringent laws regarding the importation of gold. The price of gold is therefore high in India, where gold is a passion and a status symbol. Anyone who can produce gold is sure of a good profit as long as he does not get caught. Smuggling pays; it proceeds with timetable regularity; and Dubai is a principal source of such gold.

Once a poverty-stricken sheikhdom in southeastern Arabia, Dubai is affluent by the grace of oil and a policy that permits free trade in gold, which enters and leaves as the traders see fit. Some twenty banks in Dubai handle gold, and

Gold smugglers transact business in Dubai.

the system seems to be one of ordinary commerce until you realize that it thrives on the smuggling of gold into India and, to a lesser degree, into Iran and other neighboring countries.

Much of the Dubai gold, not a native product, comes from elsewhere in the Middle East. In Beirut, Lebanon, small gold bars, so small that a dozen make a handful, are weighed, validated, stamped with a special seal, and dispatched by jet to Dubai. There they are taken aboard boats for the voyage across the Arabian Sea, during which members of the crew sew the bars into broad belts holding four rows of twenty-five each. One belt weighs 26 pounds and can be worn by a man without too much discomfort. A number of belts can be carried in a sack, the usual manner of handling this cargo since the sailors of the Dubai boats do not ordinarily go ashore in India to dispose of the gold.

161

Rather, boats come out from Bombay, the port of call, for a rendezvous at sea. The Indians return with the gold they have bought and take their chances of not being noticed and arrested, a risk worth running in order to reach the black market in gold that realizes huge profits for those who engage in it.

Another type of smuggling connects this crime with art and archaeology. Collectors and museums are constantly in the market for artifacts that are beautiful or that fill a gap in their collections, and there are men and women who do not inquire too persistently about the origin of valuable pieces that come their way. The laws are strict against the removal of national treasures, such as archaeological finds, but the international black market is a powerful magnet for smugglers, who steal gold from digs or bribe workmen to steal it for them. Occasionally a scandal exposes a smuggling operation. Ordinarily the loot passes unnoticed. Gold objects still cross borders, although not on the scale that bereft Mexico of a multitude of disks, ornaments, and figurines—Aztec treasures—in the past. Many a collector owns pieces whose provenance he does not wish to discuss.

This being the air age, smuggling and stealing involve planes, in which small amounts of gold can be quickly transferred by passengers from one place to another. To do so is becoming more difficult now that so many airports have installed electronic devices to detect metal. The precaution is against plane hijacking, to find out if anyone is carrying a gun or other weapon by means of which he might take over an aircraft, but the electronic devices pick up gold, too.

Larger amounts of gold transported by air are vulnerable to hijackers. During the 1950s two notable thefts occurred. A consignment of gold earmarked for transportation from Waterloo Air Terminal to London Airport disappeared somewhere along the line. In the second case, gold placed with other cargo aboard an Air France flight bound from Orly Airport to Geneva was missing when the plane landed.

An older form of gold theft continues, the maneuver called "higrading," which means that gold miners steal some of the gold they dig, hiding it on their persons, carrying it above ground, and selling it to fences. This is a lucrative trade when the miners can get away with it, but for those who take the metal in the form of amalgam, it also holds the danger of mercury poisoning.

Human beings are willing to risk their lives for gold. Cases are known in which they have sacrificed their lives, as did Pancho Villa's henchman who, following a bank robbery in Mexico, wandered into quicksand and sank rather than throw away the heavy gold he was carrying.

Modern-day grave robbers (opposite) in Colombia handle gold they have unearthed.

Chapter Seven
Hidden Treasure

Much of the gold in the world is lost or inaccessible, and some is merely presumed to exist; but in virtually no case is the matter allowed to lie there. A rumor is enough to trigger persistent searches by hopeful individuals who want to clear up a mystery and get rich at the same time. Gold hunters are busily at work in various places around the world at this moment. Articles in popular magazines give them hints about where to look.

Some gold, assuming it exists, is plainly beyond reach. No one is going to level Johannesburg in order to see whether a reef really does extend down into the earth below the city, which in any case is worth more than any metal that might be discovered. Johannesburg, however, is not typical of gold stories, which usually concern treasure that is at least theoretically retrievable, the problem being to find what is lost or to reach what is protected by natural obstacles.

The hunt for concealed gold in a big way begins in modern times with the Spaniards in Peru when they heard that the Incas, having been robbed in Cuzco, were taking away tremendous hoards of sacred objects from their still unpillaged temples. Atttempting to head off the treasure trains, Pizarro dispatched his men into the hinterland beyond Cuzco. They marched to Pachacamac and other cities, only to find the buildings stripped of their gold decorations. The Spaniards ravaged public buildings and brutalized their captives, but no Inca would answer questions put to him.

This sixteenth-century treasure hunt therefore failed, and so has every search since then for the missing Inca gold. It was believed for a long time that Machu Picchu, the "lost city of the Incas" deep in the Andes, might be the place of concealment. Machu Picchu was discovered in 1911 by an

The Tairona, a Colombian tribe known for its goldsmithing, created (c. 1500) this gold pendant with the unusual headdress.

American archaeologist, Hiram Bingham, who found no sign of gold. The search continues because every once in a while an archaeologist, historian, or optimistic amateur believes he might get lucky. Does the Inca gold actually exist? Or is it a fable? No one knows.

A more certain place to look for pre-Columbian gold is the Sacred Well at Chichén Itzá on the Yucatan Peninsula, once a center of the brilliant Maya culture. The Sacred Well, sixty feet deep now, probably much deeper then, is known to have been a site of human sacrifice where victims were thrown in and carried straight to the bottom by the heavy weight of the ceremonial gold ornaments they wore. Gold figurines and similar cult objects were also dropped into the water to placate the rain-god of the Maya. Centuries of such rites laid a golden "floor" in the well.

Another American, Edward H. Thompson, who, using a crude dredge and employing divers, took gold and jewels from the Sacred Well, speculated that he recovered only a small fraction of the treasure piled up down there, a thought that inspired other men to continue the search. The problem has always been that the Sacred Well cannot be drained. Water pumped out is immediately replaced, apparently because of a stream running underground through this area of Yucatan. Even archaeologists of the Mexican government, equipped with the most powerful pumps, have been unable to remove the water and allow a thorough search of the silt at the bottom. Dredges and divers continue to bring up bits and pieces from the treasure of the rain-god, but the real haul awaits someone who can figure out how to drain the Sacred Well and then compel it to surrender its fortune.

The treasure of Panama is more dubious. When Henry Morgan turned the original city into rubble during his piratical raid and could not find most of the gold for which he had come, he left feeling baffled. Mulling over the problem, he concluded that the gold had been sent away aboard ship, a lame theory since there would not have been time or opportunity between the Spaniards' discovery of his presence and the fall of the city. A more plausible theory, widely held by those interested in the subject, is that the gold was buried in tunnels that existed under the old city and were covered over by the ruins. If so, those who hid it may have been killed in the raid, may have fled somewhere else, or may have been unable to clear away the rubble when they returned. This theory is given some support by gold objects dug up in some of the tunnels when they were cleared later on. The central cache has yet to be found.

A modern mystery of Latin American gold concerns Cocos Island, 300 miles out in the Pacific from Costa Rica. In 1820, during the revolution against Spanish rule in Bolivia, the owners of an enormous accumulation of gold,

Perched high in the mountains of Peru, the extraordinary ruins of Machu Picchu show us the remains of the once-imposing Inca city.

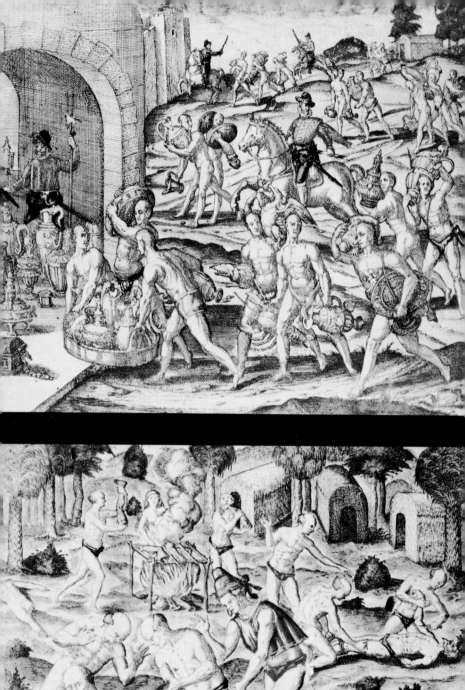

silver, jewels, and art objects, in terror of the revolutionaries, carried their wealth aboard the *Mary Dear*, whose captain, a Scot named Thompson, received orders to sail around the Horn, cross the Atlantic, and land his passengers at a Spanish seaport.

Unfortunately, Thompson and his crew were aware of the type of cargo they carried, and the knowledge proved too much for them to resist. They murdered the passengers, dumped their bodies overboard, and headed for Cocos Island, well away from civilization and its naval patrols. Here they buried their booty, which would stay put until they could safely return and recover it. That day never came. The bodies of some of their victims were recovered from the Pacific, the truth became known, and a trial followed. Thompson, escaping from jail and the noose, died in his bed after revealing to a friend the whereabouts of the treasure on Cocos Island.

The secret is said to have been handed down to a number of men who went to the island and took part of the treasure, leaving the bulk as too much or too dangerous to handle. If so, the secret vanished with the last of these men, who bequeathed to subsequent gold seekers one of their durable mysteries. Cocos Island is too big for all the possible hiding places to be dug up, and none of those tested has given so much as a clue to a hidden fortune. The island has seen much hoping and hunting, but no practical results.

Another island that belongs to the tales of hidden treasure is Oak Island off Nova Scotia. No trail of rumors or speculations led to Oak Island. On the contrary, this mystery in the lore of gold transpired entirely by accident. But it developed into the most intriguing, perplexing, long-lived, and expensive of all the mysteries.

In 1795 a sixteen-year-old boy named Daniel McGinnis was roaming the island when he spotted an oak tree with a sawn-off branch from which hung a ship's block and tackle. Below the branch, a depression in the ground showed that a hole had been dug there. Determined to find out why, he returned the next day with two friends, and the trio began to dig in the depression. They got down to ten feet and hit a platform of oak logs. Galvanized by the thought that a treasure lay just below, they took up the logs, only to discover more earth. Continuing to dig, they had the same experience at twenty and thirty feet, at which point they had to stop because emptying the hole with a bucket had become impossible.

Unable to accomplish much more on their own, the three reported at home what they had found and done. More Nova Scotians became interested, and, after an examination of Oak Island and its sawn-off oak tree, a number of leading citizens formed a company that in 1804 attacked the site with excavation machinery. They dug down ninety feet, finding every ten feet a platform of oak logs except for the next-to-last, which was of clay mixed with oil, and the last, which was of fiber matting.

At ninety feet they recovered a flat stone bearing an inscription in indecipherable symbols. Encouraged, the workers returned the next day. The hole was filled with water. They sank another shaft and joined the two in an effort to clear the first, the result being that water filled both shafts. It was salt water, showing that a subterranean channel connected the holes with the ocean. Draining the Atlantic was too tough even for a group of experts, and they went out of business.

In 1849 another company tried, drilling down to 100 feet, where the drill cut through wood and metal and came up marked by particles of gold. Fifty feet lower it bit through some inches of solid concrete. All appeared well except for the water. The company did everything it could, sinking more shafts and building a coffer dam, but nothing worked.

A similar fate awaited a number of other companies that sought to succeed where the others had failed. One group included young Franklin Delano Roosevelt, who came over to Oak Island from his nearby summer home at Campobello. FDR, his imagination quickened by the weird relics of a strange band at work on the island back in the eighteenth century, said he wanted to finish the job of digging all the

Today, almost 200 years after the discovery of the site, men continue to drill (below) and excavate (opposite) at Oak Island.

way down. He and his colleagues failed because of the water. They departed, leaving Oak Island as it was.

The puzzling questions remain unanswered. Who dug the original shaft? Pirates? Captain Kidd, perhaps? How did they do it when modern equipment cannot handle the water? Was the water table lower then? Did they break open the passage to the sea to protect their cache? Why the series of log platforms? Why the two that are not of logs? What about the stone and its unreadable inscription? To answer these would be to solve the bewildering mystery of Oak Island.

Gold mining, it might be assumed, would produce good stories of missing gold. Such is in fact the case.

During the gold rush of forty-nine, two Germans working as partners moved up along the North Fork of the American River until they found themselves in a trackless region of the mountains. They tramped through the woods, climbed hills, skirted cliffs, descended into valleys, and kept looking for the signs of auriferous rock. They found it in a vein of gold broad enough to convince them that they were on the verge of becoming millionaires.

Hastily they built a small cabin at the site, hurried to the nearest town for supplies, and set out on their return journey full of great expectations. Back in the mountains, they looked eagerly for their cabin, and looked and looked, and could not find it. For three weeks they trudged over the area searching desperately, despairingly, before agreeing that their memories were too clouded to be relied on.

Returning to town, they described their discovery and their loss, and offered to share the gold with anyone who would help them find it again. As gold strikes were being made along the American River, finding aid was easy. A search party followed the Germans back to the last point on the trail they recalled and then roamed the mountains looking for peaks they had noted overlooking the cabin. The hills eluded them and the search petered out. Later parties and individuals had no more luck. The strike reported by the Germans remains the Lost Cabin Mine of the gold rush.

Then there is the more famous Lost Dutchman Mine of the Superstition Mountains in Arizona. This one is loaded with legends. The story in outline goes like this.

During the nineteenth century, a gold mine in the mountains of the Arizona Territory east of Phoenix was worked by the Peralta family under the provisions of an old Spanish land grant. In 1864 a band of Apaches attacked the mine and massacred all who were there.

The surviving head of the family, having no stomach for working the mine himself, employed Jacob von Waltz, a German, the "Dutchman" of the tale, to do it for him. Waltz was a skilled miner and a violent man afraid of nothing. He brought in a partner, Jacob Weiser, and, defying the

Apaches, the two mined for gold, of which there was a great deal. In the 1870s, the last of the Peraltas washed his hands of the whole problem. He sold out to Waltz and Weiser, left Arizona for Mexico, and died there.

Waltz made the wealth of the mine public knowledge by coming to town with a bag of gold from time to time and spending with carefree abandon. He would never say where the mine was located, and in coming and going he craftily covered his tracks by using roundabout routes, muffling the hooves of his horse with padding, and doubling back occasionally in order to meet anybody who might be shadowing him. Several men who tried to follow him back to the mine were found shot to death in the Superstitions, crimes for which he was blamed but for which he was never prosecuted for want of evidence. Weiser vanished, killed either by Waltz or by the Apaches, after which Waltz mined his claim alone.

He concealed the mine's mouth by piling up logs, boulders, and underbrush. He stood guard with a gun. The news got around that getting too close to "the Dutchman's Mine" was dangerous. The number of interlopers he was supposed to have shot varied from six or eight to over a dozen. The picture is one of a murderous misanthropist living alone in the mountains, hacking gold from the earth with pickax and shovel, drooling over his wealth as it piled up, and reaching for his gun at the sound of a human voice or the ring of a horseshoe on a rock.

How Waltz ended remains one of the mysteries about him. Some said he died in Phoenix, others that he collapsed in the mountains and that his skeleton might one day be found. At any rate, he ceased to frequent his old haunts in town with his bags of gold, and the fact dawned in stores, saloons, and brothels that he would never be back. This meant that his mine in the mountains lay vulnerable to anyone who could find it. A scramble began. Prospectors plunged into the Superstitions, following Waltz's route as far as it was known, then striking out in different directions.

Waltz had covered his tracks too well. They all came back tired, weather-stained, and disappointed. Since then innumerable attempts have been made. The failures, too, have been innumerable. The fruitlessness of the search has caused historians of Arizona mining to doubt that this bonanza ever existed outside the imagination of Waltz's contemporaries. The reality of the man himself has been questioned. The debate continues.

So does the search. Apparently there will always be gold hunters ready to drop everything to tramp through the Superstition Mountains on the chance that they might stumble on that will-o'-the-wisp, the Lost Dutchman Mine.

Australian gold gave us the tale of Lasseter's Lost Reef. In

Overleaf: Legend has it that the Superstition Mountains in Arizona enfold the Lost Dutchman Mine.

173

1929 Harold Bell Lasseter returned from an expedition into the outback and announced that he had discovered a massive gold reef six miles long in the mountains along the border of central and western Australia. He gathered men for a new expedition, not a hard thing to do given this golden lure, and in 1930, using camels for pack animals, they moved into the interior.

At first all went well, but as Lasseter failed to locate the reef, his companions were afflicted by doubts and wondered if there was any sense in going on. Lasseter, a dogmatic individual fanatically bent on getting to the mountains where he could feast his eyes on the gold again and embarrass the skeptics, rubbed his men the wrong way so often that dissension broke out. He and they came to a parting of the ways. Lasseter in a huff took a string of camels and departed by himself into the vast isolation of the outback. The others went home.

Lasseter was never seen alive again. When he did not return, search parties went looking for him, one of which had for a scout an aborigine who claimed to have found Lasseter's body and to have buried it, and who produced letters and a diary from the camp where he made the discovery. A check of the handwriting indicated that the documents had belonged to Lasseter. Most of those who have examined the evidence believe Lasseter died of an illness brought on by the hardships, mental and physical, he encountered in his dogged effort to find his reef. He lay down at his final camp and never got up, and the Bushman who stumbled on his remains interred them nearby.

The end of Lasseter did not end speculation about his gold. Parties kept going into the outback to look for Lasseter's Lost Reef until in 1936 an Australian geologist visited the area described by Lasseter, surveyed the mountains and its rocks, and pronounced gold-bearing ore to be a scientific impossibility. The rocks he saw were sedimentary, not the igneous type that alone are auriferous. Unless there is a fallacy in the argument from geology, Lasseter threw his life away for nothing. He must have been deceived by his imagination, the victim of a mirage, when he peered through the dust and haze of the outback and told himself ecstatically that he had found gold.

South African gold gave us the tale of Kruger's missing millions. In the anarchic circumstances caused by the Boer War, when British forces invaded the Transvaal, the government of Paul Kruger was, as we have seen, the only authority capable of keeping any of the mines open. A few operated until the last moment and produced, it was said, gold amounting in value to well over £2 million. Yet strangely, when the British entered and occupied Pretoria (the capital of the Transvaal) as Kruger fled, they found no

Paul Kruger (opposite) led the South Africans in their resistance against the British and was elected president four times before he fled the country.

signs of the bullion that presumably was left over after the expenses of the war had been paid. What became of it?

That Kruger ordered its removal was testified to by one of his servants, who quoted him as saying he would take the gold to Europe and have it minted into coins, which would be used to finance further prosecution of the war. Since Kruger arrived in Europe without the gold and since it did not follow him, for he suffered from financial straits during his exile, the question of its fate arose again.

Talk became common that Kruger had had the treasure buried somewhere in the northern Transvaal. As the British imposed their rule over the whole Transvaal, rendering obsolete any plan to use the gold against them, and as Kruger's exile became permanent, ownership of "Kruger's missing millions" grew uncertain. And that was sufficient to draw adventurers into the desolate area of the Transvaal near the border with Rhodesia.

Among them was Daniel Swart, the most fantastic figure in the history of South African gold, a psychopath subject to intermittent bouts of homicidal mania. Swart, who went out first with a single partner, said on returning that they had found a skeleton and bits of gold in an isolated spot and that his partner had deserted him. The partner, failing to return and never heard from again, was Swart's first victim. There would be no point in asking the reason for the murder. A few cross words turning into an argument and then into a quarrel would have been enough to touch off an uncontrollable urge in Swart's unbalanced mind.

On the basis of his gold story, Swart raised an expedition to explore the northern Transvaal. He and his men pitched camp on a river and plodded into the wasteland. The leader, taking a companion with him, went to look for a waterhole, two shots were heard, and Swart came back alone. He said their colleague was in pursuit of a deer he had shot and would catch up with them on the trail. This individual failed to catch up for the very good reason that Swart had killed him, senselessly and oblivious to the suspicion he brought upon himself with his absurd fiction.

Phantasmagoria followed for the others, who slogged along in thirst and exhaustion. Swart pretended to go looking for the Kruger gold alone after telling his men to continue their trek. Perhaps in his crazed brain had formed the idea that it would be pleasant if they collapsed and died. This explanation is as good as any, and in keeping with Swart's reappearance, when he startled and frightened them by behaving like a wild man. Turning rational, he stated that he had found the gold. Should not they all, it was suggested, go and get it? Swart vetoed the idea on the implausible ground that the cache was too heavy for them in their weakened condition, so they must seek help in Johannesburg. They

were too tired to argue, and by now some of them wanted to be rid of Swart, who they believed was playing a game with Kruger's treasure.

Back in the city built on gold, Swart regrouped his expedition, but one member now felt something was seriously wrong. He informed the police, a search retrieved the remains of the second victim, who had been shot twice, Daniel Swart went on trial for his life, and in 1903 he finished his career by mounting the scaffold.

What actually became of the Boer gold? One theory is that the product of the Transvaal mines during the Boer War, never so great as the rumors declared, vanished in paying for the war. Another theory is that Kruger had the gold loaded aboard a merchant vessel, the *Dorothea,* at Durban. The *Dorothea* sank, carrying the missing millions to the bottom of the Indian Ocean. Then there is the possibility that they are indeed buried in the Transvaal.

The stories of misplaced gold are legion, so numerous that no single book, to say nothing of a single chapter, could describe them all. They range from ancient triremes resting on the bottom of the Mediterranean, to pirate treasure supposedly buried on islands of the Caribbean and along the coast of North America, to war treasures such as the Nazi millions that may be in Lake Toplitz and the tsarist millions that may be in Lake Baikal. To continue listing the possibilities would result in a lengthy catalogue.

One reality must be covered in even a brief account, namely, the gold that went down in Spanish treasure ships of the seventeenth and eighteenth centuries. While other vessels have had gold in their holds when they sank, the Spanish experience was unique in both the number of ships and the amount of gold they carried.

Each year galleons heavily laden with gold and silver from Spanish possessions in the New World formed long convoys for the transatlantic voyage to Cadiz. They ran a gauntlet of natural and manmade obstacles. Some suffered broken hulls when they struck rocks or reefs along the coast. Some foundered in Caribbean hurricanes or Atlantic storms. Some fell prey to pirates or privateers. Some became casualties of naval battles during the wars between the European powers. In consequence, there are no better sites to explore for missing gold than the underwater relics of the Spanish treasure fleets.

The biggest known concentration of galleons and gold lies at the bottom of Spain's Vigo Bay off the coast of Galicia, a casualty of the War of the Spanish Succession that convulsed Europe during the reign of Louis XIV. In 1702 a convoy of 19 galleons set sail from Havana loaded with gold and silver to help defray the expenses of Louis XIV and of Philip of Anjou, his grandson whom he had placed on the throne of Spain. These two monarchs were allies facing an alliance of England and Holland, two strong sea powers with fleets patrolling the Atlantic. Realizing the danger, the admiral of the Spanish convoy decided not to chance the long run down to Cadiz but to make for the security of Vigo Bay in the north, where his ships might anchor and his cargo of precious metals be taken overland to its destination.

Vigo Bay turned out to be a trap rather than a sanctuary. A combined Anglo-Dutch fleet broke through the shore defenses, attacked the escorting warships, and sank or silenced most of them. Then came the turn of the galleons. When capture was inevitable, Spanish sailors hurled chests of doubloons and pieces of eight into the bay before the English and Dutch boarded the vessels and took them in tow. Most of the galleons were hit during the battle. They sank under the pounding of the guns or were scuttled to prevent their being seized by the enemy, and came to rest about sixty feet down, so deep as to be invisible from the surface. The larger part of the treasure thus ended up in Vigo Bay. Its value may be guessed from the fact that the gold and silver in one or two galleons towed away by the British amounted to over £1 million.

The Anglo-Dutch fleet was barely gone before Philip V ordered an attempt to salvage the precious metals he needed so badly. Divers went down, but operating in deep waters, they accomplished nothing. The Spanish government then allowed individuals to try. In 1742 a Frenchman, using divers, diving bells, dredges, pontoons, and a system of cables and winches, managed to raise a vessel from the shallowest part of Vigo Bay—and suffered the disappointment of finding it a warship devoid of either gold or silver. In 1766 an Englishman recovered some pieces of eight. In 1870 a French firm recovered a small fortune in silver.

The large fortune in both metals became increasingly elusive because the tides and the weight of the water pushed the wrecks from their original sites and covered them over with mud and sand. That is why no great haul of treasure has ever been brought up, and why a salvage group exploring Vigo Bay can entertain the possibility of entering an underwater Eldorado.

When galleons went down in accessible shallow water, interest in recovering part of their gold cargoes developed very shortly. This occurred at various places in the Caribbean, and especially on the Bahama Banks, the chain of reefs flanking deep water that curves to the north of the Dominican Republic (on the island of Hispaniola), where pieces of wreckage could be discerned from the surface. Sponge divers were accustomed to plunge down onto rocky ledges and bring up handfuls of coins before any large scale recovery efforts were made.

Overleaf: The British and Dutch sent a Franco-Spanish fleet with cargoes of gold and jewels to the bottom of Vigo Bay.

*With his recovery of sunken **treasure**, Sir **William** Phips made his fortune and launched a governmental career.*

William Phips of Massachusetts, who had sailed before the mast in the Caribbean and learned of the many Spanish wrecks on the Bahama Banks, arrived there in 1687 as master of a seagoing ship with a tender for working in the dangerous shallow water. His intention was to raise an entire cargo of the precious metals, and he nearly succeeded.

His prize was the flagship of a 1641 treasure fleet forty feet below the surface. His system was to send down an experienced sponge diver carrying in his hands a stone heavy enough to drag him to the bottom in a few seconds. Alighting on the reef near the wreck, the diver scooped up coins and put them in a basket already lowered for the purpose. A tug on the rope attached to the basket started it on its way to the surface. When the need for air became critical, the diver tugged on a rope wound around his leg and crewmen immediately hauled him up.

Phips stayed for six weeks, employed a corps of divers, and recovered precious metals worth perhaps $5 million today. Sailing to England with his treasure, he impressed James II so much by his exploit that the King appointed him provost marshal in Massachusetts. Phips seemed to have reached the height of success when named the first royal governor of Massachusetts, but he became involved in the Salem witch delusion, appointed the commission that condemned victims to death on the testimony of hysterical girls, was summoned to London to explain his conduct, and died there in 1695.

No other attempts to rediscover the flagship galleon, the *Concepción*, were successful until November, 1978, when Burt Webber, a 36-year-old adventurer, located the site of the wreck and brought up some ancient artifacts that presaged recovery of the treasure.

Another current discovery concerns the *Nuestra Señora de Atocha*, which in 1622 foundered off Florida in a hurricane. Melvin Fisher, the head of a salvage company, after plotting the position of a wreck with reference to documents in the Spanish archives, concluded that he had found the *Atocha* near the Marquesas Keys. Although the identification is not absolutely certain, the cargo of the wreck squares with that known to have been aboard the galleon. Fisher's men have been bringing up gold coins, gold plate, golden ornaments, and golden religious objects in profusion.

Who owns wrecks in the sea? The finder, if the wreck is in international waters. In coastal waters, the government decides. Florida takes one quarter of the value of treasure raised in Florida waters, an important point because so many ships litter the floor of the sea off the coast of the Sunshine State.

Marine salvage has become easier in this age of scuba diving and "vacuum cleaners" that can sweep up gold from the sand. Yet the procedure is usually difficult and sometimes hazardous, depending on the combination of such factors in any particular case as time of submersion, depth of the water, temperature, tides, nature of the seabed, and conditions on the surface where salvage boats have to anchor. Salvage workers are undeterred by the difficulties. Many enter the field every year, and the chances of recovering an underwater fortune have never been better.

The amount of gold that is known to be waiting to be retrieved from the land or the sea suggests this question: May there not be great golden treasures that have dropped out of sight and out of memory and that also are waiting to be retrieved? A negative reply seems impossible considering the incredible quantities of gold that have been mined down the ages, not only in the West but also in Africa and the Orient. Gold may have been lost or buried on the Gold Coast and the Malabar Coast, in the temples of Angkor Wat and those of Sri Lanka. Gold may lie in the waters of Polynesia, Kashmir, and the Baltic islands. But there is no need to go that far afield. The Americas and their coastal shelves may hold more lost gold than has yet been discovered.

Melvin Fisher smiles as he contemplates part of the treasures he and his crews have recovered from the Caribbean depths.

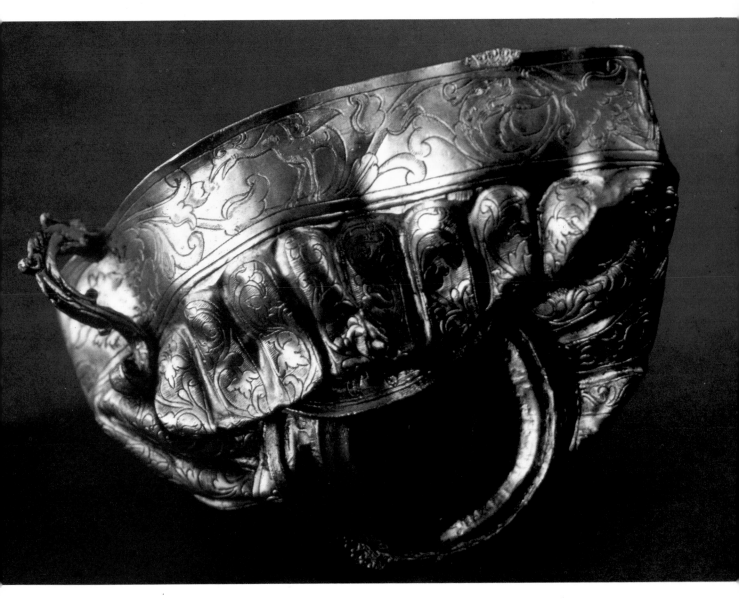

*This gold cup, once ringed inside with emeralds,
was salvaged from a wrecked Spanish ship near
Florida's Marquesas Keys.*

An earnest of wonderful things to come is at Vergina, a village in northern Greece, identified by archaeologist Manolis Andronicos with Aegae, the capital of ancient Macedonia. In 1977, Andronicos dug through a huge tumulus, or burial mound, removed a stone from a carefully walled-up tomb, peered through the aperture, and saw into an interior where gold shone amid bronze and silver. The sight did not rival that of Howard Carter at the tomb of Tutankhamen, but it was electrifying enough for Andronicos, who believed he was gazing at the final resting place of Philip II, King of Macedon.

Entering the tomb, the archaeologist discovered a large golden casket containing charred human bones, evidently the remains of the king, whose body was burned with Macedonian rites (partial cremation with charred bones ceremonially gathered and entombed). Another golden casket held the remains of a woman, presumably his second queen. Among the ornaments of the tomb were a magnificent golden quiver and a series of gold disks carved into lion heads.

The gold came from the mines of Mount Pangaeus, so abundant in the precious metal that Philip fought a campaign to gain control of them, after which he had the sinews of war for the grandiose career of conquest and expansion on which he embarked. The hoplites (armed infantrymen) of Athens and the eloquence of Demosthenes, who launched against him the speeches called "Philippics," were alike ineffectual in attempting to stop Philip's victories over the Greeks. He was the leader of Greece as well as Macedonia, and planning an invasion of Persia, when an assassin struck him down in 336 B.C. The murder may have been instigated by Olympias, his former queen whom he had repudiated when he married again; and his son by Olympias may also have been privy to the plot—Alexander the Great, who picked up where Philip left off and conquered Persia.

All previously excavated royal tombs in Macedonia had been plundered by grave robbers. Philip's may have escaped because the tumulus covered two tombs. The thieves who pillaged the first apparently did not know about the second, and so it remained untouched until a modern archaeologist excavated the entire burial mound. The identification of Philip is questioned by some experts, none of whom denies that Andronicos made a marvelous discovery, no matter who the occupant of the tomb was.

Gold has thus come to light at Vergina that was hidden before 1977; more could come to light elsewhere at any time; perhaps the future will bring as many spectacular discoveries as the past. On land and sea, the vocation of the gold seeker has not lapsed. Hope springs eternal.

The excavation site (top) at Vergina, Greece, contains a tomb thought to be that of Philip II, father of Alexander the Great. Vast treasure including vases and cups of gold and silver (bottom) was found there.

Chapter Eight
Gold Today

The story of gold can be told in many ways, one of which is to divide the story into three chapters—the artistic, the monetary, and the industrial. All three belong to the past although they have different chronologies. All three belong to the present, to the latest phase that is in full course toward a future about which guesswork would be hazardous.

The artistic use is the oldest and most basic. The esthetic sense that made prehistoric men and women decorate themselves with gold ornaments plainly belongs to human nature, which explains why the feeling is as forceful as ever it was in previous millennia. The ratio of some gold art objects to one another is a variable because of changes in the market. The crowned heads who used to order ornate pieces from goldsmiths with no thought of the expense are no longer with us, and the governments and organizations that have the money today are not interested in such things. No one is going to commission a contemporary Cellini to make something similar to the Vienna saltceller.

On the other hand, there is no slackening in the demand for gold objects within the means of ordinary people, no end to the making of gold rings, gold earrings, gold tie pins, gold watches. Much newly minted gold goes into these items, and tons of old gold are reworked and refashioned every year to produce them.

The monetary use of gold does not go back that far in the annals of humanity. It dates from the Phoenicians, who well within historic times invented money, that convenient medium by which other things can be evaluated and exchanged instead of being bartered for one another in bulk. Money has taken different forms since then, ranging from stones and shells to beads and salt, and among metals, silver

Commissioned by the Metropolitan Museum of Art, "The Sun" by Richard Lippold (opposite) is a large gold-filled wire sculpture with a rotating center.

has always been acceptable; but the best money of all has been gold. Its durability kept it from wearing out in the manner of lesser metals when passed from hand to hand. Its desirability in the marketplace was such that a small amount, easily carried, would buy a lot of goods and services. It was universally acceptable, so that any merchant or traveler could get anything he wanted, anywhere, for gold. An ancient Roman in Greece, a medieval Englishman in Spain, a nineteenth-century Russian on the Riviera, each could pay his way in gold.

While we no longer handle gold in this personal fashion, it still functions internationally as money of enormous value. The economic strength of a nation is still judged substantially by the store of bullion it possesses or controls. Except for gold, South Africa would not rank among the financial powers of the world, nor would Dubai be as significant as it is in international affairs.

The industrial use of gold is the youngest of the traditions, dating, properly speaking, no further back than the last century, when science opened a vast new market. Physicists experimenting with electricity exploited the fact that gold was a good conductor; by placing a film of gold at the connectives of an electrical system, they were able to prevent a diminution of the current flowing through these points. Gold rose in value with the rise of the electrical industry. Experiments with the vacuum produced another application of gold, as a lubricant superior to anything else. It also proved to be a shield against infrared rays. All of these uses are expanding in our time because of the space program. Gold increases the reliability of electrical apparatus in space vehicles, maintains lubrication in the vacuum that is outer space, and protects them from the infrared rays of the sun, which otherwise would raise the temperature of the interior to an intolerable degree. This last use applies to some earthbound skyscrapers that are cooled by a thin layer of gold on the windows, lowering the temperature significantly but not interfering with the passage of light through the glass.

Art and industry continue today in the gold trade in much the same sense as in the past. The main difference concerns gold as money, where different psychological and sociological laws are at work, where differences of opinion—controversies, to speak plainly—keep the place of gold in modern life in constant change.

A controversial issue is the gold standard. In the days before paper currency, gold and silver were both used as money, the former being the more valuable of the two metals such that a small amount of gold balanced a large amount of silver. The same disparity obtained in buying and selling other objects—it took less gold, more silver, to pay for a

Gold foil was used in the space program to protect astronauts and their sensitive equipment from the brutal rays of the sun.

horse, a cord of wood, or a pair of boots. Paper money, when it was introduced, derived its value from a guarantee of the issuing authority that paper could be exchanged for gold or silver, and therefore was as sound as they were.

In 1816 Great Britain went on the gold standard, meaning that pounds sterling could be exchanged for gold but not for silver. Bimetallism confused British currency because sivler fluctuated in relationship to gold (more silver being demanded for less gold) and because it deteriorated after much handling, as gold did not. Most Western nations, including the United States, followed London's example and replaced bimetallism with monometallism. The golden age of the gold standard existed between the American Civil War and World War I.

The gold standard brought stability to the monetary system of a nation by preventing the government from issuing too much paper money. Where the guarantee existed that the paper unit (dollar, pound, franc, mark, lira) could be redeemed in gold, a balance between that unit and the gold supply had to be maintained. Otherwise there might be

The landscape of Johannesburg is lined with man-made hills of crushed rock from which gold has been extracted.

demands for gold that could not be met. No government could give in to the terrible temptation to create money by spinning the printing presses, a practice that shakes confidence in the currency and leads to runaway inflation.

The gold standard suffered from a contrasting financial ailment. The amount of available gold being relatively fixed, it did not provide for sufficient flexibility in adding to the money supply. A shortage of money might slow down the economy, cause unemployment, and halt public works. Stagnation and depression in some places led to a demand for the restoration of bimetallism. In the United States, free coinage of silver became the aim of a political movement for which William Jennings Bryan spoke in 1896 with his "Cross of Gold" speech.

Silver was not returned to a significant place in monetary systems. The gold standard collapsed in the devastation of World War I and the financial crises that followed. Nations ceased to guarantee, or to permit, an exchange of gold for their currency units, and today the internal gold standard is a thing of the past.

An international gold standard remains in force because it creates stability in the monetary relations between countries. The International Monetary Fund oversees the system, which makes one large concession to internal problems: While gold remains the measure and is pegged at a given ratio to national currencies, that ratio can be shifted to help a member nation that may be suffering from a severe economic problem, such as an unacceptable inflation rate.

These are esoteric matters about which professional economists argue with no chance of reaching a consensus, much less of explaining to the uninitiated what the furor is all about. The practical implications of an international gold market are often easy enough for laypersons to understand.

One implication is that gold, like all commodities, is subject to the law of supply and demand. If gold were as common as dirt, it would be dirt cheap. If gold were as rare as a painting by Leonardo da Vinci, it would be, like the *Mona Lisa*, priced beyond any market. Gold falls between these extremes, for while it is widely distributed on the surface of the earth, the retrievable amount is limited. Gold therefore has a price, and a price that fluctuates. The only way to prevent fluctuations is to fix the price artificially.

Where gold is allowed to "float," it finds its own price level. This is what happened during the 1970s when the release of gold from its constraints caused the price to shoot up, aided by a new policy in Washington that permitted Americans to buy gold. Fixed at $35 an ounce in 1968, the price was hovering around the $200 level a decade later.

Buyers now include private citizens who go into gold as an investment, as a commodity that will continue to be of real value no matter what the fate of paper currencies, stocks, or bank accounts. All these may be shaken by bad government policies or inflation, but gold is a hedge against economic waywardness. It is the precious metal that has been good since the beginning of time and, if the past is any indication, will be good until the end of time. After all, the highest compliment that can be paid to any source of income is "as good as gold." And not many paper currencies merit that compliment anymore.

That is why so many Americans, like men and women around the globe, follow the daily gold quotations from the London Gold Market, which, on the basis of reports from the gold-producing and gold-buying centers of the world, promulgates the latest figure twice a day. The bullion may be in Johannesburg vaults or in Swiss banks under the eyes of the "gnomes of Zürich." It may stay put after transactions, the only transfer being the signs labeling the ownership of particular consignments. If, say, an American bank buys $5 million worth of gold, that cache serves the credit of the bank and does not have to be transported physically to the United States.

Some economists believe the International Monetary Fund should shift away from gold to another system, emancipating its members from the "gold bugs." The trouble is that every time the unanswerable question comes up: What else is there as practical and acceptable as gold? The United States no longer converts dollars into gold on demand, but the dollar is still defined legally in a ratio with gold; and this is a broad international practice that everyone understands.

There are dangers for individuals who invest in gold. Since the price does fluctuate, it is possible, as with most investments, to get on the wrong end of a seesaw—to buy dear and be forced to sell cheap. Again, the price of gold at a given moment may be decided, not by the marketplace working on its own, but by the manipulation of speculators in Beirut or Hong Kong. Moreover, gold can be counterfeited or given a short weight. In certain parts of the Middle East, brass is stamped as gold or the weight of a gold bar is falsified. Often only an expert in gold can detect the fraud. But gold rarely lacks buyers.

One effect of the renewed interest in gold because of its high price is the fillip given to gold mining. Geologists are again exploring for auriferous ore. The places of the famous gold rushes—California, Australia, the Klondike—saw a hiatus in mining years ago because the take had ceased to be worth the effort. Now that the same small amounts of gold are profitable, miners are back at work and the sight of a placer miner panning a stream is no longer necessarily a show for tourists or a scene for a film.

The mines that remained profitable all along are going full blast. The Homestake Mine, largest in the Western Hemisphere, which opened in Lead, South Dakota, in 1877, places around $18 million in gold on the market every year. The mines of South Africa remain at the head of the list. Competiton comes from the Soviet Union, whose gold production is a secret closely guarded by the Kremlin. Some Soviet mines are the sites of labor camps where dissidents, political prisoners, and others who defied the Moscow regime work under the dreadful conditions described by Solzhenitsyn in his *Gulag Archipelago*. Ironically, these critics of despotism have no choice but to help their adversary, the Kremlin, in its efforts to disrupt the economies of the free world by dumping gold on, or withholding it from, the international market.

Gold therefore remains valuable. It is not, nevertheless, the one ultimate treasure it was in the past. The most alluring dream one could have in this regard used to be to own a gold mine. Today it might be an oil well, and an industrial nation like the United States might well prefer to own the oil of Arabia rather than the gold of South Africa.

The famous Homestake Mine uses sophisticated machinery to extract the precious metal.

Uranium is another competitor. The future could bring more competition from scientific inventions, from new metals or alloys developed in the laboratory and better able to perform for industry the functions now monopolized by gold.

One thing that would make gold lose its value would be a glut of the precious metal, a contingency that could become a reality if hydrologists ever devise a method of extracting gold from seawater. The rivers of auriferous areas—the Sacramento, the Macquarie, the Yukon, and smaller streams—have for eons been sending their currents laced with gold through the land and on to the sea, which as a result constitutes a treasure house that contains far more gold than humanity now possesses.

Part of this gold is available through dredging. Sometimes the sea returns gold to the land, beach gold, particles of appreciable size beaten into the sand by the surf, the variety that Rex Beach pursued into the tidal zone of the Seward Peninsula in Alaska. The finest sea gold, much the largest amount, remains diluted in the water.

Naturally attempts have been made to remove it. In the most rigorous scientific endeavor, the German government after World War I dispatched an expedition out into the

Overleaf, left: Two-and-one-half miles below the surface, miners work (top) in intense heat and humidity. Hand sorters (bottom) remove lumps of non-gold bearing rock from conveyor belts that carry the ore to a crusher.

Overleaf, right: After processing with cyanide, which dissolves the gold in the water-soaked crushed ore, the separated gold solution is heated in a crucible, and the liquid gold is poured out into rough bars.

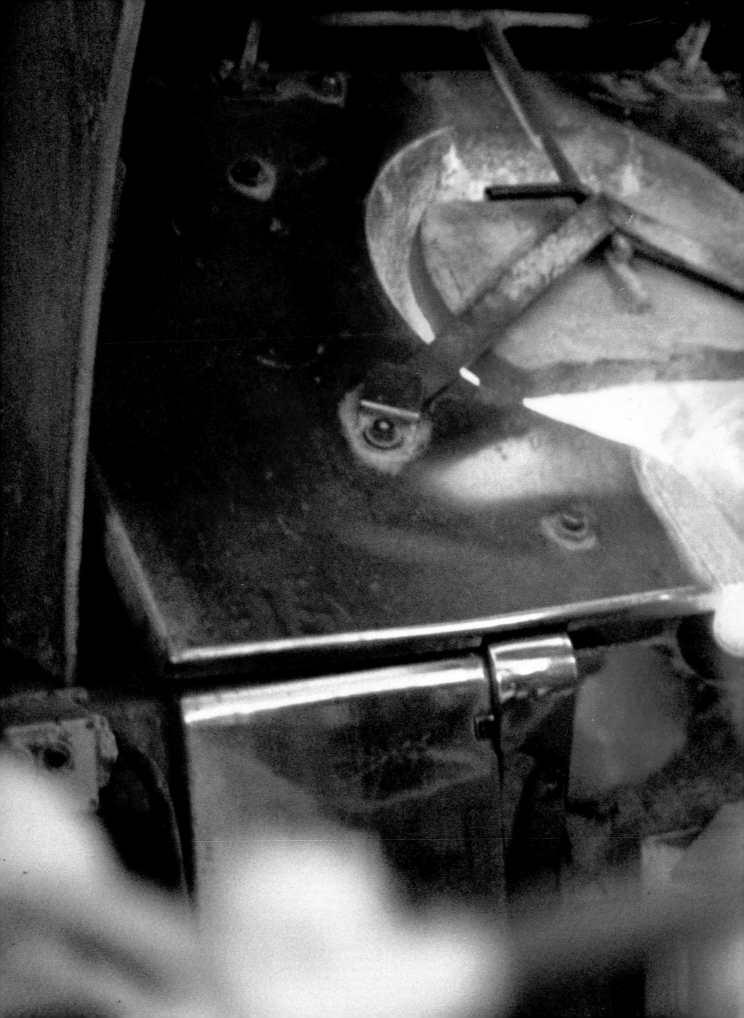

ocean to see if sufficient gold might be recovered to pay off the war debts and raise the nation to affluence again. A chemist, Fritz Haber, sailed aboard a vessel especially equipped with hydrology laboratories and filtering systems, conducted dozens of experiments, and ended with nothing practical. He reported from this voyage that every cubic mile of seawater contained gold worth hundreds of millions of marks and that to extract the gold would take 200 tanks of water, each 500 feet square and five feet deep, that would have to be filled, filtered, and emptied twice a day, the cost of which would exceed the value of any gold retrieved. Haber's judgment still stands.

Commenting on his report, Rachel Carson noted that the sea holds gold "enough in total quantity to make every person in the world a millionaire." But these millions would, in truth, be worthless, for who would sell anything for gold when he already had all the gold he wanted? Should a feasible method be discovered of straining seawater for its mineral content, the gold produced would overwhelm the gold market, undermine the value of gold, and bring the price down so drastically that the worth of gold would approximate that of wood, glass, or any commodity in plentiful supply.

One may hope it never comes to that. Gold should retain its value because it has been so dramatic a part of human experience, an almost living presence in reality and mythology, something loved as if it were a sentient being capable of reciprocating the passion. Men have sacrificed themselves to gold as if to a mistress. Women have found in gold the quintessential beauty, in "golden hair" the best of physical attributes. Nations occasionally appear mesmerized by gold not only as fortune but as good fortune.

Fort Knox is a golden symbol for the American people, the place where gold bars are heaped up within a protective system worthy of Ian Fleming (who in fact used Fort Knox as a setting for one of his James Bond thrillers). Steel, stone, and concrete outer walls encase the vault, which is protected by a steel door weighing twenty tons, by an alarm system so sensitive that it goes off at a slight change of temperature, and by photoelectric eyes. Sentries stand guard all the time, and in the area beyond the building is a whole military complex, for Fort Knox is the army's center for training in armored warfare.

Fort Knox became the bullion depository of the U.S. government in 1936. Eventually its hoard came to $20 billion, a basic factor in America's wealth when the dollar was strong, and important in slowing the decline of the dollar as it weakened.

The fame of Fort Knox is built on gold, as are Cellini's saltceller and Wagner's *Ring*. The history of California,

Preceding: The impure rough bars go to the refinery where they are processed at 1100°C., purified, and cast into bars.

Australia, the Transvaal, and the Klondike would lose much excitement were their gold rushes dropped from the record. Imagination would have less to work on without the possibility that Captain Kidd buried his treasure somewhere along the Atlantic shore or that the Lost Dutchman Mine is waiting to be found in the Superstition Mountains. Economic history is hardly ever enlivened by tragicomedy, but Jay Gould did it with gold on Black Friday.

All this is surely not fated to remain in the past. No doubt there will be future novelties unimaginable now. That the romance of humanity with gold will continue appears certain. All it will take will be the cry of "Gold!" to start another gold rush to some place as unforeseen as were, in their time, the Sacramento and the Klondike.

Gold in Literature

Historically, to use gold at all has meant to use it as lavishly, as extravagantly, as ostentatiously as possible. Early records indicate how generously it was used for royal and religious purposes.

According to Herodotus, the Greek historian writing in the fifth century B.C., more than 26 tons of gold had been used to build and furnish the legendary Tower of Babel.

Queen Hatshepsut of Egypt, who ruled from 1486-68 B.C., had two great stone pillars erected, their tops covered with gold so that, when they caught the sunlight, they appeared to be a pair of gigantic torches. The records quote her as boasting:

> To gild them I have given gold measured by the bushel, as though it were sacks of grain. You who after long years shall see these monuments will say, "We do not know how they can have made whole mountains of gold."

The Bible contains over 460 references to gold; the first, in Genesis, describes Havilah as the land "where there is gold." And gold was not to be spared in making the chest in which the tablets engraved with the Ten Commandments were to be placed. From Exodus 25:

> 10   And they shall make an ark of shittim wood; two cubits and a half shall be the length thereof, and a cubit and a half the breadth thereof, and a cubit and a half the height thereof.
> 11   And thou shalt overlay it with pure gold, within and without shalt thou overlay it, and shalt make upon it a crown of gold round about.
> 12   And thou shalt cast four rings of gold for it, and put them in the four corners thereof; and two rings shall be in the one side of it, and two rings in the other side of it.
> 13   And thou shalt make staves of shittim wood, and overlay them with gold.
> 14   And thou shalt put the staves into the rings by the sides of the ark, that the ark may be borne with them.
> 15   The staves shall be in the rings of the ark; they shall not be taken from it.
> 16   And thou shalt put into the ark the testimony which I shall give thee.

Reproduced on this page and the following pages are 19th-century engravings showing scenes in the lives of gold miners.

17   And thou shalt make a mercy seat of pure gold; two cubits and a half shall be the length thereof, and a cubit and a half the breadth thereof.

18   And thou shalt make two cherubim of gold, of beaten work shalt thou make them, in the two ends of the mercy seat.

19   And make one cherub on the one end, and the other cherub on the other end: even of the mercy seat shall ye make the cherubim on the two ends thereof.

20   And the cherubim shall stretch forth their wings on high, covering the mercy seat with their wings, and their faces shall look one to another; toward the mercy seat shall the faces of the cherubim be.

21   And thou shalt put the mercy seat above upon the ark; and in the ark thou shalt put the testimony that I shall give thee.

22   And there I will meet with thee, and I will commune with thee from above the mercy seat, from between the two cherubim which are upon the ark of the testimony, of all things which I will give thee in commandment unto the children of Israel.

23   Thou shalt also make a table of shittim wood; two cubits shall be the length thereof, and a cubit the breadth thereof, and a cubit and a half the height thereof.

24   And thou shalt overlay it with pure gold, and make thereto a crown of gold round about.

25   And thou shalt make unto it a border of an hand breadth round about, and thou shalt make a golden crown to the border thereof round about.

26   And thou shalt make for it four rings of gold, and put the rings in the four corners that are on the four feet thereof.

27   Over against the border shall the rings be for places of the staves to bear the table.

28   And thou shalt make the staves of shittim wood, and overlay them with gold, that the table may be borne with them.

29   And thou shalt make the dishes thereof, and spoons thereof, and covers thereof, and bowls thereof, to cover withal: of pure gold shalt thou make them.

30   And thou shalt set upon the table shewbread before me alway.

31   And thou shalt make a candlestick of pure gold: of beaten work shall the candlestick be made: his shaft, and his branches, his bowls, his knops, and his flowers, shall be of the same.

What female heart can gold despise?
  what cat's averse to fish?

THOMAS GRAY
"Ode on the Death of a Favourite Cat," 1748

In 1516, Sir Thomas More wrote *Utopia,* the second book of which presented an ideal society on an imaginary island, where all things, including the use of gold, were founded entirely on reason.

. . . By this trade of traffic or merchandise they bring into their own country not only great plenty of gold and silver, but also all such things as they lack at home, which is almost nothing but iron. And by reason they have long used this trade, now they have more abundance of these things than any men will believe.

. . . They keep an inestimable treasure, but yet not as a treasure, but so they have it and use it, as in good faith I am ashamed to shew, fearing that my words shall not be believed. And this I have more cause to fear, for that I know how difficult and hardly I myself would have believed another man telling the same, if I had not presently seen it with mine own eyes.

. . . They have found out a means which, as it is agreeable to all their other laws and customs, so it is from ours (where gold is so much set by and so diligently kept) very far discrepant and repugnant, and therefore incredible, but only to them that be wise. For whereas they eat and drink in earthen and glass vessels which, indeed, be curiously and properly made and yet be of very small value, of gold and silver they make commonly chamber-pots and other vessels that serve for most vile uses not only in their common halls but in every man's private house. Furthermore, of the same metals they make great chains, fetters, and gyves wherein they tie their bondmen. Finally whosoever for any offense be infamed, by their ears hang rings of gold, upon their fingers they wear rings of gold, and about their necks chains of gold, and, in conclusion, their heads be tied about with gold. Thus by all means possible they procure to have gold and silver among them in reproach and infamy. And these metals, which other nations do as grievously and sorrowfully forgo, as in a manner their own lives, if they should altogether at once be taken from the Utopians, no man there would think that he had lost the worth of one farthing.

. . . Ambassadors came to Amaurote while I was there. . . . All the ambassadors of the next countries. . . . were wont to come thither in a very homely and simple array. But the Anemolians, because they dwell far thence and had very little acquaintance with them, hearing that they were all apparelled alike, and that very rudely and homely, thinking them not to have the things which they did not wear, being therefore more proud than wise, determined in the gorgeousness of their apparel to represent very gods, and with the bright shining and glistering of their gay clothing to dazzle the eyes of the silly poor Utopians. . . . They came in cloth of gold, with great chains of gold, with gold hanging at their ears, with gold rings upon their fingers, with brooches and aglets of gold upon their caps which glistered full of pearls and precious stones, to be short, trimmed and adorned with all those things which among the Utopians were either the punishment of bondmen or the reproach of infamed persons or else trifles for young children to play withal.

SIR THOMAS MORE
Utopia, 1516

The story of Atahualpa, the Inca of Peru, includes, quite literally, the offer of a king's ransom in gold. In 1532, on his third expedition to Peru, Francisco Pizarro reached the city of Cajamarca and captured the unsuspecting Indian monarch. To secure his freedom, Atahualpa offered to have a vast treasure of gold and silver objects delivered to the Spaniard. Pizarro accepted, but after the ransom was received, instead of releasing the Inca, Pizarro brought him to trial on a dozen charges, among them ordering the murder of his half-brother (a rival for the throne) and plotting against the Spaniards. Atahualpa was executed in the great square of Cajamarca in August 1533.

It was not long before Atahualpa discovered, amidst all the show of religious zeal in his Conquerors, a lurking appetite more potent in most of their bosoms than either religion or ambition. This was the love of gold. He determined to avail himself of it to procure his own freedom. . . .

Appealing to the avarice of his keepers, he one day told Pizarro that if he would set him free he would engage to cover the floor of the apartment on which they stood with gold. Those present listened with an incredulous smile; and, as the Inca received no answer, he said, with some emphasis, that "he would not merely cover the floor, but would fill the room with gold as high as he could reach;" and, standing on tiptoe, he stretched out his hand against the wall. . . . [Pizarro] acquiesced, drawing a red line along the wall at the height which the Inca had indicated. . . . The apartment was about seventeen feet broad, by twenty-two feet long, and the line round the walls was nine feet from the floor. This space was to be filled with gold; but it was understood that the gold was not to be melted down into ingots, but to retain the original form of the articles into which it was manufactured, that the Inca might have the benefit of the space which they occupied. He further agreed to fill an adjoining room of smaller dimensions twice full with silver, in like manner; and he demanded two months to accomplish all this.

No sooner was this arrangement made than the Inca despatched couriers to Cuzco and the other principal places in the kingdom, with orders that the gold ornaments and utensils should be removed from the royal palaces, and from the temples and other public buildings, and transported without loss of time to Cajamarca.

[It came:] goblets, ewers, salvers, vases of every shape and size, ornaments and utensils for the temples and the royal palaces, tiles and plates for the decoration of the public edifices, curious imitations of different plants and animals. Among the plants, the most beautiful was the Indian corn, in which the golden ear was sheathed in its broad leaves of silver, from which hung a rich tassel of threads of the same precious metal. A fountain was also much admired, which sent up a sparkling jet of gold, while birds and animals of the same material played in the waters at its base. . . .

The division of the treasure was agreed upon. . . . It was necessary to reduce the whole to ingots of a uniform standard, for the spoil was composed of an infinite variety of articles, in which the gold was of very different degrees of purity. . . .

The business of melting down the plate was intrusted to the

Indian goldsmiths, who were thus required to undo the work of their own hands. They toiled day and night, but such was the quantity to be recast that it consumed a full month.

WILLIAM HICKLING PRESCOTT
The Conquest of Peru, 1847

One of the most famous gold sculptures of all time is the saltcellar made, in the early 1540s, by Benvenuto Cellini for Francis I of France. In his autobiography, Cellini gives us a first-hand (and typically egotistical) account of how the work came to be designed and how it was received.

In Paris, the king . . . sent for me . . . His majesty immediately began to talk to me, saying that since he had so beautiful a cup and basin of my making, he must have a handsome salt-cellar to accompany such fine things; that he wanted me to draw a design of one, and the sooner the better. I answered that his majesty should see such a design much sooner than he expected; for that whilst I was employed about the basin and the cup, I thought a salt-cellar would be a necessary companion to them, and therefore had already made one, which I should show to his majesty in a few moments. . . . He then told me he would be glad to see my design.

I went for it; and soon returned, for I had nothing to do but to cross the Seine: I brought with me the model of wax, which I had made at Rome at the request of the Cardinal of Ferrara. Upon showing it to the king, he expressed great surprise, and said, "This is a much finer design than I expected; it is a most noble production; such a genius should never be unemployed." He turned to me, and said with great cheerfulness, that he was highly pleased with my model, and should be glad to have a salt-cellar made according to it in gold. The Cardinal of Ferrara winked at me, giving me to understand that he knew this to be the same model I had made for him in Rome. . . . The king asked me how much gold the making of the salt-cellar would require. I immediately answered him, a thousand crowns. The king called for his treasurer . . . and commanded him to give me directly a thousand gold crowns, good weight. . . .

About the time that I had completely finished it, the king was returned to Paris: I paid him a visit, carrying the salt-cellar with me, which . . . was of an oval figure, and in size about two thirds of a cubit, being entirely of gold, and admirably engraved by the chisel. . . . I had represented the sea and the earth both in a sitting posture, the legs of one placed between those of the other, as certain arms of the sea enter the land, and certain necks of the land jut out into the sea. The manner in which I designed them was as follows: I put a trident into the right hand of the figure that represented the sea, and in the left a bark of exquisite workmanship, which was to hold the salt; under this figure were its four sea-horses, the form of which in the breast and fore feet resembled that of a horse, and all the hind part from the middle that of a fish; the fishes' tails were entwined with each other in a manner very pleasing to the eye, and the whole group was placed in a striking attitude. This figure was surrounded by a variety of fishes of different species, and other sea animals. The undulation of the water was properly exhibited, and likewise enamelled with its true colours. The earth I represented by a beautiful female figure holding a cornucopia in her hand, entirely naked, like the male figure; in her left hand she held a little temple, the architecture of the Ionic order, and the workmanship very nice; this was intended to put the pepper in. Under this female figure, I exhibited most of the finest animals which the earth produces, and the rocks I partly enamelled and partly left in gold. I then fixed the work on a base of black ebony of a proper thickness; and there I placed four golden figures in more than mezzo rilievo: these were intended to represent Night, Day, Twilight, and Dawn. There were also four other figures of the four principal winds, of the same size, the workmanship and enamel of which were elegant to the last degree.

When I showed the king this piece of work, he burst into an exclamation of surprise, and could never sufficiently admire it.

BENVENUTO CELLINI
Autobiography, c. 1560

Four hundred years ago, the gold mines in what is now Mozambique and Rhodesia were part of the Portuguese empire. A contemporary report on the mining methods in use at that time was given by the Portuguese historian and crown administrator João de Barros.

In those Manica mines, . . . the [Kaffirs] have to labour hard, the land being so dry; for all the gold found there is in dust, so that they have to take the excavated earth to a place where water can be had, for which they make some holes where it collects in winter, and generally nobody digs more than six or seven spans deep [four to five feet], and if they go to twenty they come upon hard rock.

[In] other mines, the gold is found of larger size, some embedded in the reefs, some already cleared by the winter torrents; hence, in some of the pools, such as remain in summer, they dive down and find much gold in the mud brought up. In other places, where are some lagoons, two hundred men set to work to drain off about half the water, and in the mud which they sift they also find gold; and so rich is the ground that if the people were industrious great quantities could be had; but they are so indolent that stress of hunger alone will keep them in the mines. Hence the Moors who visit these districts have recourse to a ruse to make them diligent. They deck the negroes and their women with clothes, beads, and trinkets, in which they delight, and when all are pleased, trust everything to them, bidding them to go and work the mines, and on their return at such a time they can pay for those things; so that in this way, by giving them credit, the Moors induce them to work, and so truthful are the negroes that they keep their word.

JOÃO DE BARROS
Décadas da Ásia, 1552-1563

The art of alchemy produced a great variety of rogues, including those who claimed to have found "the philosopher's stone" and those who sought to enrich themselves by buying it. Ben Jonson's play *The Alchemist* satirizes many of them. The play is prefaced by an amusing device, an acrostic that summarizes the action to come.

ARGUMENT

T *he sickness hot, a master quit, for fear,*
H *is house in town, and left one servant there;*
E *ase him corrupted, and gave means to know*

A *Cheater, and his punk; who now brought low,*
L *eaving their narrow practice, were become*
C *ozeners at large; and only wanting some*
H *ouse to set up, with him they here contract,*
E *ach for a share, and all begin to act.*
M *uch company they draw, and much abuse,*
I *n casting figures, telling fortunes, news,*
S *elling of flies, flat bawdry with the stone,*
T *ill it, and they, and all in the fume are gone.*

Mammon. Come on, sir. Now, you set your foot on shore
in *Novo Orbe;* here's the rich Peru:
And there within, sir, are the golden mines,
Great Solomon's Ophir! he was sailing to't,
Three years, but we have reach'd it in ten months.
This is the day, wherein, to all my friends,
I will pronounce the happy word, BE RICH;
THIS DAY YOU SHALL BE SPECTATISSIMI.
You shall no more deal with the hollow dye,
Or the frail card . . .
And unto thee I speak it first, BE RICH.

. . .

>   . . . This night, I'll change
> All that is metal, in my house, to gold:
> And, early in the morning, will I send
> To all the plumbers and the pewterers,
> And buy their tin and lead up; and to Lothbury
> For all the copper.

BEN JONSON
The Alchemist, 1610

William Kidd was a British privateer who turned pirate, was tried for piracy and murder, and was hanged in 1701. The legend of his buried treasure kindled the imagination of Edgar Allen Poe, one of the geniuses of American letters. In his fanciful short story "The Gold Bug," Poe tells of the successful search for these long-lost riches on Sullivan's Island, near Charleston, South Carolina.

    . . . In a few seconds [the dog] had uncovered a mass of human bones, forming two complete skeletons, intermingled with several buttons of metal, and what appeared to be the dust of decayed woollen. One or two strokes of a spade upturned the blade of a large Spanish knife, and, as we dug further, three or four loose pieces of gold and silver coin came to light. . . .

    We now worked in earnest, and never did I pass ten minutes of more intense excitement. During this interval we had fairly unearthed an oblong chest of wood, . . . three feet and a half long, three feet broad, and two and a half feet deep. It was firmly secured by bands of wrought iron, riveted, and forming a kind of open trellis-work over the whole. On each side of the chest, near the top, were three rings of iron—six in all—by means of which a firm hold could be obtained. . . . Our utmost united endeavors served only to disturb the coffer very slightly in its bed. We at once saw the impossibility of removing so great a weight. Luckily, the sole fastenings of the lid consisted of two sliding bolts. These we drew back—trembling and panting with anxiety. In an instant, a treasure of incalculable value lay gleaming before us. As the rays of the lanterns fell within the pit, there flashed upward a glow and a glare, from a confused heap of gold and jewels, that absolutely dazzled our eyes. . . .

    The chest had been full to the brim, and we spent the whole [next] day, and the greater part of the next night, in a scrutiny of its contents. There had been nothing like order or arrangement.

Everything had been heaped in promiscuously. Having assorted all with care, we found ourselves possessed of even vaster wealth than we had at first supposed. In coin, there was rather more than four hundred and fifty thousand dollars—estimating the value of the pieces, as accurately as we could, by the tables of the period. There was not a particle of silver. All was gold of antique date and of great variety—French, Spanish, and German money, with a few English guineas, and some counters, of which we had never seen specimens before. There were several very large and heavy coins, so worn that we could make nothing of their inscriptions. There was no American money. The value of the jewels we found more difficulty in estimating. There were diamonds—some of them exceedingly large and fine—a hundred and ten in all, and not one of them small; eighteen rubies of remarkable brilliancy;—three hundred and ten emeralds, all very beautiful; and twenty-one sapphires, with an opal. These stones had all been broken from their settings and thrown loose in the chest. The settings themselves, which we picked out from among the other gold, appeared to have been beaten up with hammers, as if to prevent identification. Besides all this, there was a vast quantity of solid gold ornaments; nearly two hundred massive finger and ear rings; rich chains—thirty of these, if I remember; eighty-three very large and heavy crucifixes; five gold censers of great value; a prodigious golden punch-bowl, ornamented with richly chased vine-leaves and Bacchanalian figures; with two sword-handles exquisitely embossed, and many other smaller articles which I can not recollect. The weight of these valuables exceeded three hundred and fifty pounds avoirdupois; and in this estimate I have not included one hundred and ninety-seven superb gold watches; three of the number being worth each five hundred dollars, if one. Many of them were very old, and as timekeepers, valueless; the works having suffered, more or less, from corrosion—but all were richly jewelled and in cases of great worth. We estimated the entire contents of the chest, that night, at a million and a half of dollars; and upon the subsequent disposal of the trinkets and jewels (a few being retained for our own use), it was found that we had greatly undervalued the treasure.

EDGAR ALLEN POE
"The Gold Bug," 1843

When every blessed thing you hold
Is made of silver, or of gold,
    You long for simple pewter.
When you have nothing else to wear
But cloth of gold and satins rare,
For cloth of gold you cease to care—
    Up goes the price of shoddy.

SIR WILLIAM SCHWENCK GILBERT
"The Gondoliers," 1889

The cry of "Gold!" was enough to put whole communities in turmoil. On May 29, 1848, the California town of Monterey got word of the discovery at Sutter's Mill, and it was never the same again. Walter Colton—a journalist, teacher, and minister, who had gone to California as a United States Navy chaplain—was serving as alcalde in Monterey at the time. His extensive journals contain detailed reports of everyday life that summer.

Tuesday, June 20.—My messenger, sent to the mines, has returned with specimens of the gold; he dismounted in a sea of upturned faces. As he drew forth the yellow lumps from his pockets and passed them around among the eager crowd, the doubts, which had lingered till now, fled. . . . The excitement produced was intense; and many were soon busy in their hasty preparations for a departure to the mines. The family who had kept house for me caught the moving infection. Husband and wife were both packing up; the blacksmith dropped his hammer, the carpenter his plane, the mason his trowel, the farmer his sickle, the baker his loaf, and the tapster his bottle. All were off for the mines, some on horses, some on carts, and some on crutches; and one went in a litter. An American woman who had recently established a boardinghouse here pulled up stakes, and was off before her lodgers had even time to pay their bills. Debtors ran, of course. I have only a community of women left, and a gang of prisoners, with here and there a soldier, who will give his captain the slip at the first chance. I don't blame the fellow a whit; seven dollars a month, while others are making two or three hundred a day! That is too much for human nature to stand.

Saturday, July 15.—The gold fever has reached every servant in Monterey; none are to be trusted in their engagement beyond a week, and as for compulsion, it is like attempting to drive fish into a net with the ocean before them. . . .

Tuesday, July 18.—Another bag of gold from the mines and another spasm in the community. It was brought down by a sailor from Yuba River and contains a hundred and thirty-six ounces. It is the most beautiful gold that has appeared in the market; it looks like the yellow scales of the dolphin, passing through his rainbow hues at death. My carpenters, at work on the schoolhouse, on seeing it, threw down their saws and planes, shouldered their picks, and are off for the Yuba. Three seamen ran from the *Warren*, forfeiting their four years' pay; and a whole platoon of soldiers from the fort left only their colors behind. . . .

Saturday, August 12.—My man Bob, who is of Irish extraction, and who had been in the mines about two months, returned to Monterey four weeks since, bringing with him over two thousand dollars, as the proceeds of his labor. Bob, while in my employ, required me to pay him every Saturday night, in gold, which he put into a little leather bag and sewed into the lining of his coat, after taking out just twelve and a half cents, his weekly allowance for tobacco. . . . I met Bob today and asked him how he got on. "Oh, very well," he replied, "but I am off again for the mines." "How is that, Bob? You brought down with you over two thousand dollars; I hope you have not spent all that; you used to be very saving. . . ." "Oh, yes," replied Bob, "and I have got *that* money yet; I worked hard for it; and the devil can't get it away; but the two thousand dollars came aisily by good luck, and has gone as aisily as it came." Now Bob's story is only one of a thousand like it in California, and has a deeper philosophy in it than meets the eye. Multitudes here are none the richer for the mines. He who can shake chestnuts from an exhaustless tree, won't stickle about the quantity he roasts.

Tuesday, August 28.—The gold mines have upset all social and domestic arrangements in Monterey; the master has become his own servant, and the servant his own lord. The millionaire is obliged to groom his own horse, and roll his wheelbarrow, and the hidalgo—in whose veins flows the blood of all the Cortes—has to clean his own boots! . . . Why, is not this enough to make one wish the gold mines were in the earth's flaming center, from which they sprung? Out on this yellow dust! It is worse than the cinders which buried Pompeii, for there high and low shared the same fate!

Saturday, September 16.—The gold mines are producing one good result; every creditor who has gone there is paying his debts. Claims not deemed worth a farthing are now cashed on presentation at nature's great bank. This has rendered the credit of every man here good for almost any amount. Orders for merchandise are honored which six months ago would have been thrown into the fire. There is none so poor, who has two stout arms and a pickaxe left, but he can empty any store in Monterey.

WALTER COLTON
My Three Years in California, 1852

There are over 250 references to gold in the works of William Shakespeare. They include this description of Cleopatra, one of the most lush word pictures ever written:

The barge she sat in, like a burnish'd throne,
Burn'd on the water; the poop was beaten gold,
Purple the sails, and so perfumed, that
The winds were love-sick with them; the oars were silver,
Which to the tune of flutes kept stroke, and made
The water, which they beat, to follow faster,
As amorous of their strokes. For her own person,
It beggar'd all description; she did lie
In her pavilion,—cloth-of-gold of tissue,—
O'er picturing that Venus, where we see
The fancy out-work nature; on each side her
Stood pretty dimpled boys, like smiling Cupids,
With divers-colour'd fans, whose wind did seem
To glow the delicate cheeks which they did cool
And what they undid, did.

WILLIAM SHAKESPEARE
Antony and Cleopatra, c. 1607

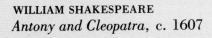

In 1849, "Punch," the London periodical of humor, entertained its readers with this satirical view of the California gold miner.

THE CALIFORNIAN OUTFIT.

Now Natur's comin' out, I guess,
And puttin' on her vernal dress;
The blooms on shrub and tree as blows
Looks like their go-to-meetin' clothes.
And lawful heart! when I behold
The sun tinge them young leaves with gold,
My thoughts to Californy turns,
The land where every crittur earns
Off his own hook, the least to say,
A hundred dollars in a day.
But he as to the Diggins goes
In course must have a suit of clothes;
Well, at our store we sell the best—
Hat, jacket, trousers, boots, and vest:
But this ain't all you'll want—oh no!
If you to Californy go.
You'll want
  A RIFLE,
            Just to keep
Your Diggins clear. We sell 'em cheap.
At good five hundred yards they kill,
In hands as "draws the bead" with skill.
  A PAIR OF GOOD REVOLVERS
              Too,
Is indispensable to you,
To give your fellow-labourers plums,
To rob your pillow when they comes.
We do 'em at the lowest figure,
Jist only try one—pull the trigger.
  A BOWIE KNIFE
             You'll also need.
Ours are the best—they are, indeed.
  A DIRK,
        Besides, you'll useful find,
To pink a feller in the wind.
The best and cheapest we affords,
And likewise recommends our
  SWORDS,
Which, if you comes for to our shop,
I estimate you'll find first chop.
This is the Outfit for the Diggins
You gets at HEZEKIAH HIGGINS'.

Charles Robert Thatcher was born in Bristol, England, in 1831. In 1853, he took his passage to Victoria where he tried gold prospecting but soon returned to his former profession as a musician. A few years later he was being advertised as the "highly popular delineator of colonial life." According to a contemporary Bendigo, Australia, correspondent, Thatcher's songs of the miners, "if circulated in England, would give a much better idea of life at the goldfields than most of the elaborately written works upon them do."

All gold had been proclaimed the property of the crown, and all diggers were required to purchase licenses. "Where's Your License?" describes the reaction of the diggers on hearing the cry "Joe," the signal that the police were engaged in one of their frequent visits to find and punish illegal prospectors.

The morning was fine
The sun brightly did shine,
The diggers were working away;
When the inspector of traps,
Said now my fine chaps,
We'll go licence hunting today.

Some went this way, some that,
Some to Bendigo Flat,
And a lot to the White Hills did tramp,
Whilst others did bear
Up toward Golden Square,
And the rest of them kept round the camp.

Each turned his eye,
To the holes close by,
Expecting on some down to drop;
But not one could they nail,
For they'd give 'em leg bail—
Diggers ain't often caught on the hop.

The little word Joe,
Which most of you know,
Is a signal the traps are quite near;
Made them all cut their sticks,
And they hooked it like bricks,
I believe you, my boys, no fear.

Now a tall, ugly trap,
He espied a young chap,
Up the gully a-cutting like fun;
So he quickly gave chase,
But it was a hard race,
For, mind you, the digger could run.

Down the hole he did pop,
While the bobby up top,
Says, "Just come up," shaking his staff—
"Young man of the Crown,

If yer wants me come down,
For I'm not to be caught with such chaff."

Of course you'd have thought,
The sly fox he'd have caught,
By lugging him out of the hole;
But this crucher no fear,
Quite scorned the idea,
Of burrowing the earth like a mole.

But wiser by half,
He put by his staff,
And as onward he went sung he—
When a cove's down a drive,
Whether dead or alive,
He may stay there till doomsday for me.

Samuel Clemens (better known as Mark Twain), the American humorist and social observer, traveled to the goldfields
of California and South Africa. In *Roughing It,* he describes
the nearly deserted mining camps in the aftermath of the
gold rush of forty-nine.

By and by, an old friend of mine, a miner, came down from one
of the decayed mining camps of Tuolumne, California, and I went
back with him. We lived in a small cabin on a verdant hillside,
and there were not five other cabins in view over the wide expanse
of hill and forest. Yet a flourishing city of two or three thousand
population had occupied this grassy dead solitude during the
flush times of twelve or fifteen years before, and where our cabin
stood had once been the heart of the teeming hive, the centre of
the city. When the mines gave out the town fell into decay, and in
a few years wholly disappeared—streets, dwelling, shops,
everything—and left no sign. The grassy slopes were as green and
smooth and desolate of life as if they had never been disturbed.
The mere handful of miners still remaining, had seen the town
spring up, spread, grow and flourish in its pride; and they had
seen it sicken and die, and pass away like a dream. With it their
hopes had died, and their zest of life. They had long ago resigned
themselves to their exile, and ceased to correspond with their
distant friends or turn longing eyes toward their early homes.
They had accepted banishment, forgotten the world and been
forgotten of the world. They were far from telegraphs and railroads,
and they stood, as it were, in a living grave, dead to the events that
stirred the globe's great populations, dead to the common
interests of men, isolated and outcast from brotherhood with their

kind. It was the most singular, and almost the most touching and melancholy exile that fancy can imagine. One of my associates in this locality, for two or three months, was a man who had had a university education; but now for eighteen years he had decayed there by inches, a bearded, rough-clad, clay-stained miner, and at times, among his sighings and soliloquizings, he unconsciously interjected vaguely remembered Latin and Greek sentences—dead and musty tongues, meet vehicles for the thoughts of one whose dreams were all of the past, whose life was a failure; a tired man, burdened with the present, and indifferent to the future; a man without ties, hopes, interests, waiting for rest and the end.

In Tuolumne lived two miners who used to go to the neighboring village in the afternoon and return every night with household supplies. Part of the distance they traversed a trail, and nearly always sat down to rest on a great boulder that lay beside the path. In the course of thirteen years they had worn that boulder tolerably smooth, sitting on it. By and by two vagrant Mexicans came along and occupied the seat. They began to amuse themselves by chipping off flakes from the boulder with a sledge-hammer. They examined one of these flakes and found it rich with gold. That boulder paid them $800 afterward. But the aggravating circumstance was that these "Greasers" knew that there must be more gold where that boulder came from, and so they went panning up the hill and found what was probably the richest pocket that region has yet produced. It took three months to exhaust it, and it yielded $120,000. The two American miners who used to sit on the boulder are poor yet, and they take turn about in getting up early in the morning to curse those Mexicans—and when it comes down to pure ornamental cursing, the native American is gifted above the sons of men.

MARK TWAIN
Roughing It, 1872

No gold rush was more difficult than the trek to the Yukon, and no one conveyed that better than Jack London. In his popular short stories, London revealed the dark cruelty of nature and the fierce characters of the men who defied her in their frenzied quest for gold.

From "To the Man on the Trail"

Crack! Crack! They heard the familiar music of the dog whip, the whining howl of the Malemutes, and the crunch of a sled as it drew up to the cabin. Conversation languished while they waited the issue.

"An old-timer; cares for his dogs and then himself," whispered Malemute Kid to Prince as they listened to the snapping jaws and the wolfish snarls and yelps of pain which proclaimed to their practiced ears that the stranger was beating back their dogs while he fed his own.

Then came the expected knock, sharp and confident, and the stranger entered. Dazzled by the light, he hesitated a moment at the door, giving to all a chance for scrutiny. He was a striking personage, and a most picturesque one, in his Arctic dress of wool and fur. Standing six foot two or three, with proportionate breadth of shoulders and depth of chest, his smooth-shaven face nipped by the cold to a gleaming pink, his long lashes and eyebrows white with ice, and the ear and neck flaps of his great wolfskin cap loosely raised, he seemed, of a verity, the Frost King, just stepped in out of the night. Clasped outside his Mackinaw jacket, a beaded belt held two large Colt's revolvers and a hunting knife, while he carried, in addition to the inevitable dog whip, a smokeless rifle of the largest bore and latest pattern. As he came forward, for all his step was firm and elastic, they could see that fatigue bore heavily upon him. . . .

"When'd yeh leave Dawson?"

"Twelve o'clock."

"Last night?"—as a matter of course.

"Today."

A murmur of surprise passed round the circle. And well it might; for it was just midnight, and seventy-five miles of rough river trail was not to be sneered at for a twelve hours' run.

From "An Odyssey of the North"

". . . 'It is the mouth of hell,' he said; 'let us go down.' And we went down.

"And on the bottom there was a cabin, built by some man, of logs which he had cast down from above. It was a very old cabin, for men had died there alone at different times, and on pieces of birch bark which were there we read their last words and their curses. One had died of scurvy; another's partner had robbed him of his last grub and powder and stolen away; a third had been mauled by a bald-face grizzly; a fourth had hunted for game and starved—and so it went, and they had been loath to leave the gold, and had died by the side of it in one way or another. And the worthless gold they had gathered yellowed the floor of the cabin like in a dream.

"But his soul was steady, and his head clear, this man I had led thus far. 'We have nothing to eat,' he said, 'and we will only look upon this gold, and see whence it comes and how much there be. Then we will go away quick, before it gets into our eyes and steals away our judgment. And in this way we may return in the end, with more grub, and possess it all.' So we looked upon the great vein, which cut the wall of the pit as a true vein should, and we measured it, and traced it from above and below, and drove the stakes of the claims and blazed the trees in token of our rights. Then, our knees shaking with lack of food, and a sickness in our bellies, and our hearts chugging close to our mouths, we climbed the mighty wall for the last time and turned our faces to the back trip."

JACK LONDON
The Son of the Wolf, 1900

Acknowledgments and Picture Credits

The Editors would like to express their particular appreciation to the following organizations and individuals:

A la Vieille Russie

Paul Schaffer

Australian Consulate, New York

Geoffrey Dixon

International Gold Corporation

Leslie Mirin

Mitchell Library, Sidney

Suzanne Mourot

Wells Fargo Bank History Room

Elaine Gilleran

The title or description of each picture appears after the page number. The following abbreviations are used in the picture credits:

BB	Brown Brothers
BL	Bancroft Library, University of California
EPA-S	Editorial Photo Archives--Scala
HUW	E. A. Hegg Photograph, U. of Washington
IGC	International Gold Corporation
LC	Library of Congress
MMA	Metropolitan Museum of Art
MLS	Mitchell Library, Sidney
NLC	National Library of Australia, Canberra
NYPL,RBD	New York Public Library, Rare Book Division

Endpapers

Detail from gilded shrine of Tutankhamen, Egyptian, 18th Dynasty. Egyptian Museum, Cairo.

Title Page

Gold second coffin of Tutankhamen, Egyptian, 18th Dynasty. Egyptian Museum, Cairo (John Ross). 6, 7—Simone Martini, *The Annuniciation*, 1333. Uffizi (Giraudon).

Chapter One

8—Night Battle of Kay Shusrow and Afrasiyab, *Shahnameh*, Persian, 16th century. MMA, Gift of Arthur Houghton, Jr., 1970. 10—top, Michael Maier, *Secretioris Naturae*, Frankfurt, 1687; bottom, George Agricola, . . . *de Re Metalica*, Basle, 1556. 11—Sir John Pettus, *Fleta Minor*, London, 1686. All: NYPL, Astor, Lenox and Tilden Foundations. 12—Ioanes Stratensis, *The Alchemist*, Flanders, 1570. Palazzo Vecchio, Florence (EPA-S). 14, 15—Alchemist's laboratory. NYPL, Picture Collection. 17—Titian, *Danae* . . ., Prado (Giraudon). 18—Jason and the Golden Fleece, red-figure krater, Athens, 5th century. MMA, Harris Brisbane Dick Fund, 1934. 19—top, English noble, 1360; bottom, Two Byzantine and early Christian coins. All: MMA, Gift Darius Ogden Mills, 1904. 20—top, Funerary mask, Pre-Columbian, Peru. Gold Museum, Bogota (IGC); bottom, Funerary mask of Tutankhamen, Egyptian, 18th Dynasty. Egyptian Museum, Cairo (John Ross). 21—Mask of Agamemnon, Mycenaean. National Archaeological Museum, Athens (EPA-S). 22—Scythian helmet, Greek, 4th century B.C. Hermitage. 23—top left, Pectoral, lion, Thracian, 5th century B.C.; top right, Rhyton, he-goat, Thracian, 4th century B.C. Both: Archaeological Museum, Plovdiv; right, Scythian comb, Greek, 4th century B.C. Hermitage. 24—top, Cope fastening. Cathedral Treasury, Aachen (EPA-S); bottom, Cross, Visigothic, 7th century. Archaeological Museum, Barcelona (Giraudon). 25—Tiara of Constance of Aragon. Duomo, Palermo (EPA-S). 26—Book cover, Archangel Michael, Byzantine, 10th century. Treasury of St. Mark's, Venice (EPA-S). 27—Illumination of Alexius I Comnenus, Byzantine, 11th century. Vatican Library, Ms. Grec. 666, fol 2v. 28—Bronze Buddha, gilt-covered, Chinese, T'ang Dynasty. MMA, Rogers Fund, 1943. 30—Benvenuto Cellini, *Saltcellar*, Kunsthistorisches Museum, Vienna (Jonathan Wright). 31—Embroidered shield of Charles IX, France, 16th century. Louvre (EPA-S). 32—Icon of Our Lady of Vladimir, Russian, 17th century. A la Vieille Russie. 33—Carl Fabergé, Imperial egg, Moscow, 1897. Collection Wartski, London (Michael Holford). 34—Shwe Dagon, Rangoon, Burma. 35—Indian bridesmaid. Both: Jonathan Wright.

Chapter Two

36—Albertis Browere, *The Gold Miner*. National Cowboy Hall of Fame. 38—Wells Fargo Bank History Room. 39—top, Samuel Osgood, *John A. Sutter*. M. H. De Young Memorial Museum; bottom, National Archives 40—BL. 41—top, New-York Historical Society; bottom, State Street Bank and Trust Company, Boston. 42—Museum of the City of New York. 43—top, New-York Historical Society; bottom, Historical Society of York County. 44—LC. 45—All: Huntington Library. 46—Los Angeles County

Museum of Natural History. 47—BL. 48—BL. 49—California State Library. 50, 51—LC. 52 & 53—All: BL except: 53 upper left, Minnesota Historical Society; lower right, NYPL. 55—top, NYPL, Prints Division; bottom, New-York Historical Society. 57—NYPL, Prints Division. 59—LC. 60—California Historical Society. 61—BL. 62—LC. 63—MMA, The Hawes Family, 1937. 64, 65—BL, Smithsonian Institution; 65, Huntington Library. 66—California State Library. 67—Wells Fargo Bank History Room.

Chapter Three

68—T. T. Balcombe, *Edward Hargraves*, 1851. MLS. 71—S. C. Brees, *How to . . . Settle in Australia*, London, 1856. NLC. 72—S. T. Gill, *Fair Prospects*, 1852. NLC 73—E. Tulloch, *Camp at Bathurst*. MLS. 74, 75—George Rowe, *Old Bendigo*, 1857. MLS. 76, 78—S. T. Gill, *Sketches of the Victorian Gold Diggings*, 1853. All: NLC. 80—Australian Information Bureau. 81—NLC, Humphrey Collection. 82—NLC. 83—J. B. Henderson, *Eureka Stockade Riot*, Ballarat, 1854. MLS. 84–87—top, Photographs by Beaufoy Merlin, 1870's. All: MSL, Holtermann Collection; 87 bottom, NLC.

Chapter Four

88—Culver Pictures. 90—Africana Museum, Johannesburg. 91—BB. 92—Africana Museum, Johannesburg. 93—BB. 95—Both: BB. 96 & 97—Both: Satour. 98—Radio Times Hulton. 100—Radio Times Hulton. 101—BB. 102—Radio Times Hulton. 102—inset, U.S. Army. 103—LC. 105—Collection Sirot, Paris.

Chapter Five

106—LC. 108—Culver Pictures. 109—National Archives. 110—LC. 111—HUW. 113—HUW. 114—BB. 116—LC. 117—top, HUW; bottom, BL. 118, 119—BL. 120–23—LC. 124–128—HUW. 129—Roger Viollet, Paris. 130—National Film Board of Canada. 131 & 132—HUW. 133—National Film Board of Canada. 134—BL. 137—HUW.

Chapter Six

138—Charles Johnson, *A general History of . . . Pyrates*, 1724, NYPL,RBD. 140–143—All: MMA, Egyptian Expedition. 144 & 145—Theodore de Bry, *America*, 1590. NYPL,RBD. 146—National Maritime Museum, Greenwich 147—top, Both: Hulsius, *Voyages*, 1603. NYPL,RBD; bottom, Walter Bigges, *Expeditio Francisci Draki*, 1588. NYPL,RBD. 148 & 149—All: Exquemelin, *Bucaniers of America*, 1684. NYPL,RBD. 150—Charles Johnson, A general History of . . . Pyrates, 1724. 151—

Radio Times Hulton. 152—Both: Wells Fargo Bank History Room. 153—Bettmann Archive. 154 & 155—All: Wells Fargo Bank History Room. 156—BB. 157—top, BB; bottom, LC. 158, 159—Bettmann Archive. 161—John Perkins-Woodfin Camp. 162—Adam Woolfitt-Susan Griggs, Ltd.

Chapter Seven

164—Pre-Columbian pendant, Tairona, Colombia. MMA, Gift of Bache Foundation, 1968. 167—Susan McCartney-Photoresearchers. 168—Both: Theodore de Bry, *America*, Frankfurt, 1590. 169—Florentine Codex. Biblioteca Laurenziana, Florence. 170 & 171—Nova Scotia Information Centre. 174, 175—Bernie Schoenfield-Woodfin Camp. 177—Africana Museum, Johannesburg. 179—Culver Pictures. 180, 181—Ludolf Bakjuizen, *Battle of Vigo Bay*, 1702. National Maritime Museum, Greenwich. 183—Wide World. 184—Don Kincaid. 185—Both: Wide World.

Chapter Eight

186—Richard Lippold, *The Sun*, 1953-56. MMA. 189—NASA (IGC). 190—Information Center of South Africa. 193—Courtesy Homestake Mine. 194–197—All: IGC. 199—Information Center of South Africa.

Gold in Literature

201–216—Illustrations from LC, NYPL, NLC, California Historical Society.

Index

Page numbers in italics refer to illustrations

Abbey, James, 44
Acrisius, King of Argus, 16, 17
Aeneid (Virgil), 10
Alaska, 10
    Klondike goldfields (map), 109
    search for gold in, 107–137
Alchemist, The (Jonson), 207–208
Alchemy, 10–15
Alexander III, Tsar of Russia, 32
Alexander, the Great, 23, 185
Alexandria, Egypt, 10
Allen, Eugene, 130
Anderson, Judith, 18
Andronicus, Manolis, 185
Annunciation (Martini), 6–7
Apartheid, 91
Aqua regia, 16
Argonauts of 'Forty-Nine, The
    (Leeper), 40
Art, gold in, 19–33, 187
Australia, search for gold in,
    68–89
Athena, 17
Autobiography (Cellini), 205–206

Bao Dai, Emperor of Vietnam,
    160
Barnato, Barnett, 90–91, 97
Bart, Black, 153, *155*
Beach, Rex, 107, 136, 193
Beit, Alfred, 97
Bentley, James, 82–83
Berry, Clarence, 134
Bible, gold in, 9, 35, 201–202
Black, Martha, 116, 121
Blackbeard, *138*
Bok, Edward, 94
Bolton, Charles, 154
Bonney, Anne, 150

Boyle, Robert, 14
Boyle's law, 14
Bruff, J. Goldsborough, *45*
Bryan, William Jennings, 190
Buffum, Edward G., 49

California, 10
    search for gold in, 37–67
Call of the Wild (London), 107
Carboni, Raffaelo, 84, 85
Carmac, George W., *108*, 110,
    112, 134, 135
Carson, Kit, 37
Carson, Rachel, 198
Carter, Howard, 141, 185
Carpentier, Georges, 135
Cellini, Benvenuto, 29–30,
    205–206
Chaplin, Charles, 132
Charlemagne, 24
Charles IV, Emperor, Holy
    Roman Empire, 10
Charles IX, King of France, 30
Charlie, Tagish, 110, 112, 134
Chichen Itzá, 166
China, 29
Clacy, Ellen, 76
Clemens, Samuel L., 67,
    100–101, 214–215
Cleopatra, 35
Coins, gold, 19
Colton, Walter, 210–211
Concepción (ship), 183
Conquest of Peru, The (Prescott),
    204–205
Columbus, Christopher, 32
Comstock Lode, 66, 100
Coronado, Francisco Vasquez
    de, 10

221

Cortez, Hernando, 32
Crabtree, Lotta, *62*, 63, 66
Craig, William, 77
Croesus, King of Lydia, 18, 19
Cyrus, the Great, King of Persia, 18

Dalton, Charles and Grant, *152*
Dalton Gang, 152
Dana, Richard Henry, 43
Danaë, 16
Danaë (Titian), *17*
Dawson, Yukon Territory, 129–136
Demosthenes, 185
Dempsey, Jack, 67, 135
De Villiers, Joseph, 93
Dionysus, 17
Dorothea (ship), 178
Drake, Francis, 10, 144
Dubai, 160–161
Dyes, cloth, 14

Eldorado, 16
Eldorado (Taylor), 40
Elizabeth I, Queen of England, 143–144
Enterprise (ship), *41*
Ether, 15
Euripides, 18

Fabergé, Peter Carl, 32, *33*
Farouk, King of Egypt, 160
Fisk, "Jubilee" Jim, *156*, 157
Flagstad, Kirsten, 18–19
Flying Cloud (ship), 43
Forrest, Robert and William, 99
Fort Knox, 198
Fossickers. *See* Australia, search for gold in
Francis I, King of France, 29
Frazer, James, 10
Frederick, the Great, King of Prussia, 14
Fremont, John C., 37
Frobisher, Martin, 144
Fuggers, the, 15

Garland, Hamlin, 107, 112
Gates, Swiftwater Bill, 134
George IV, King of England, 69
Germain, Thomas, 14, 30–31
Ghana, 29
Gilbert, William S., 209
Gill, S. T., 77
Gold
  alchemists and, 10–15
  crimes involving, 139–168 *See also* Hidden Treasure
  discovery of, 9 *See also specific locations*
  hidden, 164–185
  history of, 19–35
  in Alaska, 107–137
  in art, 19–33, 187

in Australia, 68–89
in California, 37–67
in literature, 201–215
in mythology, 16–19
in seawater, 193, 198
in South Africa, 89–105
in the Bible, 9, 35, 201–202
industrial use of, 188
lure of, 9–15, 32–35
mining of, 47–49
minting of, 19
monetary use of, 187, 188–193
properties of, 15–16
rings, 35
salvaging, 178–179, 182–183
Gold Mining (Currier and Ives), *50–51*
Gold Rush (motion picture), 132
Gold standard, 188–191
Golden Ass, 10
Golden Fleece, legend of, 18
Golden Hind (ship), 10, 144
Golden Legend, 10
Golden Treasury, 10
Goldsmiths, 19–32 *See also individual artists*
Gould, Jay, 157
Grant, Ulysses S., 157
Grauman, Sid, 135
Grave-robbing, 139–143
Greek vase, Fifth century B.C., *18*
Gulag Archipelago (Solzhenitsyn), 192

Haber, Fritz, 198
Hargraves, Edward, 70–72, 73, 74, 86, 107
Harte, Bret, 56
Hartford (ship), *42*
Hatshepsut, Queen of Egypt, 10, 35
Hawkins, John, 144
Hearst, George, 66
Hearst, William Randolph, 67

Henderson, Robert, 110, 112, 134
Hidden treasure, 164–185 *See also* Gold, crimes involving
History of gold, 19–35
Holden, Helen, 135
Homestake Mine, 192
Hotham, Charles, 82, 85
Humphrey, Isaac, 47–48

Iliad (Homer), 20
India, 29
International Monetary Fund, 191, 192
"Irish Dick", 61
Istanbul, 10

James, Frank, *153*
James, Jesse, 152, *153*

James II, King of England, 182
Jane, Calamity, 131
Japan, 29
Jason, 18
Jeppe, Julius, 97
Jim, Skookum "Strong", 110, 112, 126, 134
Johannesburg, 93–94
Jonson, Ben, 14, 207–208

Kidd, William, 172
Kimberley, Duke of, 90
Klondike. *See* Alaska
Klondike Nugget, The (newspaper), 130–131, 133, 135–136
Kruger, Paul, 92, 93, 176–178
Kublai Khan, 29

Lalor, Peter, 84, 85, 86
Lamont, Thomas, 103
Lasseter, Howard B., 176
Lavoisier, Antoine, 14
Leeper, David R., 40
Lippert, Edouard, 97
Literature, gold in, 201–215 *See also individual books and authors*
Lomore, Gussie, 134
London, Jack, 107, 114, 125, 132, 215–216
Lost Dutchman Mine, 172–173, 176
Louis XIV, King of France, 178–179
Louis XV, King of France, 14, 30
Louvre, 30
Lowe, Dick, 134

Machu Picchu, 165–166
Marais, Peter, 89–90
Maria Theresa, Queen of Hungary and Bohemia, 14
Marie Antoinette, 35
Marie de Medici, Queen of France, 30
Mark Twain. *See* Clemens, Samuel L.
Marshall, James, 38–39, 58, 66, 107
Martini, Simone, 6–7
Marx, Groucho, 67
Mary Dear (ship), 169
Maspero, Gaston, 143
MacArthur, John, 99
MacArthur-Forrest cyanide process, 99–100
McBrian, James, 69
MacDonald, Alexander, 133
McGinnis, Daniel, 170
Medea, 18
Medea (Euripides), 18
Medusa, 16
Metropolitan Museum of Art, 24
Mexico, 10

Midas, King of Phrygia, 17–18
Miller, Joaquin, 107, 131
Miner's Ten Commandments, The, 58
Mining camps
  conditions in, 58–63, 76, 79–85, 94, 126–137
  women in, 63–66, 76–77, 133
Mona Lisa (Vinci), 191
Montez, Lola, *62*, 63, 66, 77
Montezuma, King of the Aztecs, 32
More, Thomas, 203
Morgan, Henry, *149*, 166
Mother Lode, 47
Murieta, Joaquin, *60*, 61, 151
My Three Years in California (Colton), 210–211

Neumann, Sig, 97
New York Daily Tribune, 44
Nome, Alaska, 136–137
Nuestra Señora de Atocha (ship), 183

Ogilvie, William, 112
Ophir, 10
Oppenheimer, Ernest, 103, 104

Panama Canal, 43
Paracelsus, 15
Peralta Family, 172–173, 176
Perseus, 16–17
Peru, 10
Philip II, King of Macedon, 185
Philip II, King of Spain, 143–144
Philosopher's stone, 13–14
Phips, William, *179*, 182
Pierce, Hiram, 54
Piracy, 144, 150
Pitman, Key, 135
Pizarro, Francisco, 32
Poe, Edgar Allen, 208–209
Polk, James K., 40
Polo, Marco, 29
Pompeii, 10
Prague, 10
Prescott, William H., 204–205
"Puffers", 13

Rackam, Jack, 150
Ramses IX, Pharoah of Egypt, 141
"Rattlesnake Dick", 61, 151
Read, Mary, 150
Rede, Robert, 83, 84, 85
Reid, Frank, 115
Residenz Museum, Munich, 24
Rhinegold, The (Wagner), 19
Rhodes, Cecil, 90–92, 93, 97, 100, 101
Rickard, T. A., 114
Rickard, Tex, 135
Ring of the Nibelung (Wagner), 18–19

Rings, gold, 35
Roosevelt, Franklin D., 19, 170, 172
Roosevelt, Theodore, 43
Ross, Charles, 84, 85
Roughing It (Clemens), 214–215
Royce, Josiah, 45
Royce, Sarah, 45, 63
Rudd, Charles, 97–98

Saltcellar (Cellini), *30*
San Francisco, 10
Schliemann, Heinrich, 20–22
Sculpture, gold. *See* Goldsmiths
Scythians, 23–24
Service, Robert, 107, 129, 137
Shakespeare, William, 211
Shah-nameh (Book of Kings), *8*
Shwe Dagon Pagoda, Rangoon, Burma, *34*
Siegfried (Wagner), 19
Skagway, Alaska, 113–114
Smith, Jefferson Randolph "Soapy", 114–115
Smuggling, 160–161, 163
Smuts, Jan C., *102*, 103
Solomon, King of the Israelites, 10
Solzhenitsyn, Alexander, 192
Son of the Wolf, The (London), 216
South Africa, search for gold in, 89–105
Spoilers, The (Beach), 107
Strauss, Levi, 54
Sun, The (Lippold), *186*
Sutter, John A., 37–38, 57
Swart, Daniel, 177–178

Taylor, Bayard, 40, 43, 54–55

Thomas, Lowell, 67
Thompson, Edward H., 166
Trail of Ninety-eight, 107
Troy (ancient), 10, 20, 23
Turpin, Dick, 151
Tutankhamen, Pharoah of Egypt, 9, 20, 185
  death mask, *20*
  second coffin of, *142*
  tomb, *141*
Twilight of the Gods, The (Wagner), 19
Two Years Before the Mast (Dana), 43

Utopia (More), 203

Valkyries, The (Wagner), 19
Vern, Frederick, 84, 85
Vinci, Leonardo da, 191
Virgil, 10
Virginia City Territorial Enterprise (newspaper), 67

Wagner, Richard, 18–19
Walker, George, 91, 107
Waltz, Jacob von, 172–173, 176
Washington, Martha, 35
Weiser, Jacob, 172
Wimmer, Jennie, 39
Women in the mining camps, 63–66, 76–77, 133
Wooley, Leonard, 139

Younger Brothers, 15
Yukon Belle (ship), 125

Zeus, 16
Zog, King of Albania, 160